Testimonio

Testimonio

On the Politics of Truth

John Beverley

University of Minnesota Press
Minneapolis · London

Chapter 1 was first published in *Modern Fiction Studies* 35, no. 1 (spring 1989): 11–28; reprinted here with the permission of *Modern Fiction Studies* and its publisher, The Johns Hopkins University Press. Chapter 2 was first published in *boundary 2* 18, no. 2 (summer 1991): 1–21; copyright 1991 Duke University Press; all rights reserved; reprinted with permission from Duke University Press. Chapter 3 was first published in Georg M. Gugelberger, ed., *The Real Thing: Testimonial Discourse and Latin America* (Durham, N.C.: Duke University Press, 1996), 266–86; copyright Duke University Press; all rights reserved; reprinted with permission from Duke University Press. Chapter 4 first appeared in Arturo Arias, ed., *The Rigoberta Menchú Controversy* (Minneapolis: University of Minnesota Press, 2001), 219–36.

Published by the University of Minnesota Press
111 Third Avenue South, Suite 290
Minneapolis, MN 55401-2520
http://www.upress.umn.edu

Library of Congress Cataloging-in-Publication Data

Beverley, John.
　　Testimonio : on the politics of truth / John Beverley.
　　　　p.　　cm.
　　Includes bibliographical references and index.
　　ISBN 0-8166-2840-8 (HC : alk. paper) — ISBN 0-8166-2841-6 (PB : alk. paper)
　　1. Reportage literature, Spanish American—History and criticism. 2. Spanish American prose literature—20th century—History and criticism.　3. Menchú, Rigoberta. *Me llamo Rigoberta Menchú y así me nació la conciencia.*　4. Politics and literature—Latin America.　I. Title.
　　PQ7082.P76B48 2004
　　868'.6080998—dc22
　　　　　　　　　　　　　　　　　　　　　　　　　　　　2003025126

Printed in the United States of America on acid-free paper

The University of Minnesota is an equal-opportunity educator and employer.

12　11　10　09　08　07　06　05　04　　　　　　　10　9　8　7　6　5　4　3　2　1

There is not just signification or interpretation. There is also truth.

—*Alain Badiou,* L'Être et l'Événement

There is no history, there are only historians.

—*Peter Greenway*

Contents

Preface

The four essays included in this volume constitute a record of my involvement over the past fifteen years with the narrative form called in Latin American Spanish *testimonio* (testimonial narrative would be the closest English equivalent). Beyond correcting typographical errors and anachronisms, updating the notes, and adding an introduction, I have resisted the impulse to revise them. Although I would not always put things in the same way today, I thought it better to leave the essays as they originally appeared for the record (with only minor changes): *quod scripsi scripsi.* In that way, I hope, the reader might be able to see my engagement with testimonio as an evolving, open-ended one, contingent, like the form itself, on the vicissitudes of history. For, as my remarks on David Stoll will indicate, I am also part of the story.

Those vicissitudes include principally the end of the Cold War. In 1989, when the first of these essays appeared, the Soviet Union still existed, Cuba had not entered its "special period in times of emergency," and the Sandinistas were still in power in Nicaragua. Despite the growing indications that something was not right with the project of socialism, it still seemed plausible—if only in the mode of Gramsci's slogan "pessimism of the intellect, optimism of the will"—to end that essay, as I did, with the claim that "if the novel had a special relationship with humanism and the rise of the European bourgeoisie, testimonio is by contrast a new form of narrative literature in which we can at the same time witness and be a part of the emerging culture of an international proletarian/popular-democratic subject in its period of ascendancy."

The "popular-democratic" after the slash was, of course, a way of hedging my bet with Marxism, but not too much so. Generally speaking, protagonists of testimonio in the Cold War years, like myself, saw it as a narrative form linked closely to national liberation movements and other social struggles inspired by Marxism. By contrast, the skeptics or antagonists of testimonio (some of them former leftists) often resorted to what amounted to a kind of "red-baiting"—the McCarthyite tactic of disqualifying someone's ideas by the allegation that he or she was a Communist or sympathetic to Communism—unless, of course, the particular testimonio in question, say Solzhenitsyn's *Gulag Archipelago* or Reinaldo Arenas's *Before Night Falls*, fit their ideological agenda, in which case it was, of course, true and compelling.

Today the context in which testimonio is read and debated is not the Cold War but globalization, not a bipolar world but one dominated by U.S. military and geopolitical hegemony, not national liberation movements or big Communist parties but the so-called new social movements, often operating at sub- or supranational levels. In this regard, my choice of *I, Rigoberta Menchú*, which was first published in 1982—a year that, in retrospect, seems a turning point—by the Cuban cultural center Casa de las Américas, to represent testimonio in these essays was fortuitous, albeit in some ways accidental. Menchú's text had a Janus-like character. On the one hand, it was produced out of a general revolutionary upsurge in Central America that had won power in one country, Nicaragua, and that at the time was bidding for power in both Guatemala and El Salvador. As such, it harked back to the genre of guerrilla testimonio, modeled above all on Che Guevara's *Reminiscences of the Cuban Revolutionary War,* and designed to win support and recruits for the various guerrilla *focos* that appeared in the wake of the Cuban Revolution, theorized by Régis Debray in his famous or (depending on one's point of view) infamous manual *Revolution in the Revolution* (Menchú's interlocutor was the Venezuelan anthropologist Elisabeth Burgos, who at the time was married to Debray; and Menchú herself was affiliated with one of the major Guatemalan guerrilla groups, the Ejército Guerrillero de los Pobres [EGP, Guerrilla Army of the Poor]). On the other hand, in its affirmation of Mayan indigenous culture and society, and its attention to women's empowerment, Menchú's testimonio looked forward to the emerging "identity politics" of the new social movements that came to occupy the place of the revolutionary left in the 1980s. Via the public debate stirred by its incorporation in the reading list of one of the Western Culture tracks at Stanford, *I, Rigoberta Menchú* also became one of the centerpieces of the "culture wars" around the issue of multiculturalism in the United States.

I had been active in the late 1970s and early 1980s in solidarity work with the Central American revolutionary movements. That experience led me to think of doing a book, in collaboration with my friend Marc Zimmerman, who had worked on cultural matters for the Sandinistas in the early years of the revolution, about the new kinds of literature produced by those movements, foremost among them testimonial narratives of various sorts. When we discussed how to write our chapter on those narratives, I got the job of trying to theorize testimonio as a new kind of literary genre. I picked Menchú's book as a paradigm. I don't remember exactly why. It was a compelling story, vividly told, and it was already, in Ann Wright's English translation published by Verso, in wide circulation in the United States at the time. But there were other choices that were equally compelling and appropriate for that purpose: for example, *Miguel Mármol*, the story, told in his own words, of a trade-union militant and founder of the Salvadoran Communist Party, compiled by the writer-revolutionary Roque Dalton; or Omar Cabezas's popular account of his experiences as a Sandinista guerrilla, *Fire from the Mountain*, which reproduced the conventions of the Cuban-style guerrilla testimonio. My attempt to define testimonio as a genre in that chapter became, in turn, the starting point of the first of the essays in this collection, "The Margin at the Center," which was published in 1989 and went on to be one of the nodal points in the widespread discussion of testimonio that ensued in the U.S. academy in the 1990s. Our book, *Literature and Politics in the Central American Revolutions,* on the other hand, came out just after the Sandinistas lost power in 1990, and promptly headed for the remainder shelves.

In retrospect, I can see now that my choice of *I, Rigoberta Menchú* to represent testimonio was determined, above all, by my sympathy for and involvement with feminism (the New Left group I had been a part of in the 1970s described itself as "socialist-feminist"; the genre of "militant" or guerrilla testimonio was predominantly male-centered, and, in a sublimated way, *machista*). But there was another matter related to "identity" too in this choice. Zimmerman and I were concerned in *Literature and Politics* to understand the involvement of people like Menchú and her family in the armed struggle in Guatemala. Guatemalan indigenous groups had been, on the whole, impervious or hostile to earlier guerrilla activities carried out basically by ladino (that is, Spanish-speaking, non-indian) Marxist activists in the 1960s.[1] What had changed since then? How had the left rethought the "indian question," as it was called, to make its message more appealing to indigenous people? What was the connection between indigenous values and interests, such as those Menchú describes in her narrative, and the new revolutionary upsurge in Guatemala? Did indigenous people become revolutionaries in spite of their previous worldviews, or because of them? We also wanted to at least register some of the controversies around indigenous rights and autonomy that came up in Sandinista Nicaragua. Those aims led us to begin to take seriously, although still in a relatively untheoretical way, concepts of history and culture that no longer depended on, to use Jean-François Lyotard's well-known phrase, the "grand narrative" of Western modernity and modernization, be this in a Marxist or a liberal form. As the voice of a singular subject, testimonio was almost by definition a *petit récit,* or, in Ranajit Guha's phrase, "the small voice of history."

It was that concern that led me to my subsequent involvement with the question of postmodernism, and to my growing interest in the new perspectives about political and cultural agency developing in postcolonial and subaltern studies. Testimonio was my point of entry into subaltern studies in particular, and the third and fourth of these essays reflect my involvement, between 1992 and 2002, with what came to be known as the Latin America Subaltern Studies Group (the Introduction, on the other hand, was written after the disbanding of the group in 2001). Subaltern studies came out of Marxism but it also proposed a fundamental revision of classical Marxism, particularly around its insistence on a singular or monistic historical teleology. In a Latin American context, this permitted a move beyond dependency theory, which was the economic "base," so to speak, of the account of cultural dynamics and agency we had given in our book on Central American revolutionary literature (I try to bring out some of the issues involved at greater length in my Introduction). My interest in postmodernism and subaltern studies was a way of both mourning and reflecting critically on the reasons for the defeat or collapse of the illusion of radical social change in Latin America and the United States I had shared with the protagonists of testimonio.

But there was also a strictly academic question involved here too. Zimmerman and I came from the field of literary criticism (we had both studied with Fredric Jameson at the University of California San Diego in the late 1960s). *Literature and Politics* was concerned with explaining how the way in which what conventionally counts as literature—poems, essays, novels—became a crucial "ideological practice," to recall Louis Althusser's term, of the Central American revolutionary movements. In that sense, our book remained within the disciplinary boundaries of literary criticism. But the question of testimonio and its role in those movements also brought us to the need to look at the limits of literature as a cultural institution. Was it in fact the case that literature—even the sort of progressive, left-nationalist literature represented by Central American writers such as Roque Dalton, Gioconda Belli, or Ernesto Cardenal—could adequately "represent" (both politically and mimetically) a subaltern social subject, whose identity as such was in part founded on an awareness of not being part of what the Uruguayan critic Ángel Rama called, in one of the most influential books of Latin American cultural criticism in the 1980s, the "lettered city" (the theme of Rama's book was that from colonial times onward, literature had been linked intimately with the power in Latin America)? In a way similar to what happened, at roughly the same time, with cultural studies, testimonio tended to destabilize disciplinary boundaries: Was testimonio in fact literature? In what section of a library or bookstore should a testimonio be placed (the answer would be different for different testimonios)? Who was the author of a text like *I, Rigoberta Menchú*: the compiler or the narrator? And if testimonio seemed to appear at the margin of literature in forms sanctioned more by the social sciences such as "life history" or "oral history," it also displaced the authority of historical and ethnographic writing (Mary Louise Pratt described testimonio, memorably, as auto-ethnography). Zimmerman and I concluded our chapter on testimonio in *Literature and Politics,* and the book itself, with the thought that while "literature has been a means of national-popular mobilization in the Central American revolutionary process, . . . that process also elaborates or points to forms of cultural democratization that will necessarily question or displace the role of literature as a hegemonic cultural institution."

We did not have to wait long to see what this opening to the future portended, but it was not at all what we imagined when we wrote those words: in 1990, just as our book came out, the Sandinistas were voted out of power by an electorate exhausted by the contra war and the economic collapse precipitated by the blockade imposed on Nicaragua by the Reagan administration (John Negroponte, the man in charge, from his position as U.S. ambassador to Honduras, of the contra war and the wider campaign to defeat or contain the revolutionary tide in Central America, is now George W. Bush's ambassador to the United Nations). That defeat marked the end of the revolutionary possibility of the Latin

American left, if not of the left itself. It is that defeat and the question of where to go from there that mark the third and fourth essays in this collection, both of which involve centrally David Stoll's well-known book on Rigoberta Menchú, *Rigoberta Menchú and the Story of All Poor Guatemalans* (Boulder, Colo.: Westview Press, 1999).

It was my friend Julio Ramos who first brought to my attention that, the same year as the Sandinistas lost power, at a conference on the theme "'Political Correctness' and Cultural Studies" at the University of California, Berkeley, where he taught, a young anthropologist named David Stoll had raised questions about the factual veracity of some of the details in Menchú's *testimonio*. Stoll and I subsequently came into contact, if memory serves me well, through the mediation of a mutual friend, Michael Taussig. I asked Stoll if I could see a copy of his Berkeley talk, in preparation for a talk of my own on *testimonio* I was scheduled to give at the 1991 meeting of the Latin American Studies Association (LASA) in Washington, D.C. As it happened, that meeting was also to be attended by Stoll himself, and by both Rigoberta Menchú and one of the generals most closely involved with the counterinsurgency war in Guatemala whose effects she describes in her narrative.

Stoll makes this occasion one of the defining moments in his book eight years later. Here is part of his account (dare I say *testimonio*?) of what transpired:

> Worried about what to do with my findings [about the discrepancies in Menchú's testimonio], I consulted with an authority on testimonio named John Beverley. Beverley was an advocate for the genre, but he also seemed to be arguing against interpreting it like a fundamentalist interprets the Bible. Perhaps he could help me frame my doubts about *I, Rigoberta Menchú* in a more sympathetic way. After an exchange of drafts, he called up and asked if he could quote me, for a presentation he was giving at the upcoming meetings of the Latin American Studies Association. At this point I had presented my argument just once, at a conference at Berkeley the previous fall, and had no interest in publishing. But not wanting to censor the flow of information, after only a moment's hesitation I said, Why not?
>
> The room at a conference hotel near Washington, D.C., was crowded with professors of literature. I slipped into the back just as Beverley began to speak. This was not my neck of the academic woods; the level of abstraction was beyond me. Suddenly Beverley swooped down from the clouds and dropped his bomb—my unfortunate findings about the death of [Menchú's brother] Petrocinio. Gasps and "no's" escaped

from some of the audience. Meanwhile, who should be holding forth in an auditorium below but the cult figure herself, who was often an honored guest at these occasions. Not having intended to make a declaration, suddenly I was in a fix. Since Rigoberta would hear that an anthropologist was bad-mouthing her upstairs, I had no choice but to present her with a copy of the twelve-page talk Beverley had quoted. When I caught up with Rigoberta in a corridor, it was hard to exchange more than a few sentences without being interrupted by the next well-wisher. But I was able to give her a copy, along with a verbal explanation that people in Chajul were giving me another version of how her brother died. Rigoberta was cordial, but I remember her saying that just as I had my work, she had hers, which I took to be a polite suggestion to avoid interfering with it. If the people of Chajul were collaborating with the [Guatemalan] army, why should I believe what they say? (Stoll, 226–27)

Stoll goes on to observe in a tone that is somewhat less congenial: "What I viewed as the main issue—how outsiders were using Rigoberta's story to justify continuing a war at the expense of peasants who did not support it—was entirely missing from Beverley's presentation. . . . Beverley and his colleagues have been promoting testimonio in a way that does not allow questioning its reliability" (241–42). I take this to mean that, when the kid gloves of academic courtesy are taken off, Stoll feels that I was not just a "literary scholar," as he likes to call me in his book, whose expert opinion he was asking for, but part of the very problem he was trying to analyze: that is, one of the "outsiders" using Menchú's testimonio, and others like it, to promote their own political agendas. I reply in kind here. (For the record, I was sympathetic to the goals of the armed struggle in Guatemala, and elsewhere in Latin America, if not always to this or that specific form of struggle, and I did see my critical-theoretical work as in some way contributing to those goals.)

But Stoll and I were not initially at odds with each other. As he notes, I had myself argued in "The Margin at the Center" that there was a creative or "storytelling" element involved in the construction of testimonial narratives, and I had been criticized on that score for "aesthetifying" testimonio at the expense of its political and ethical urgency. I thought that the way Menchú told her story was not separate from its political effect. So I was interested in the questions Stoll was asking. They seemed to echo in some ways the concerns about the representation of the subaltern my then colleague at the University of Pittsburgh, Gayatri Spivak, had raised some years earlier in her essay "Can the Subaltern Speak?"

Spivak's apparently paradoxical answer to her own question in that essay had been, No, not as such, because if the subaltern could speak in a way that really mattered to us, that we would feel compelled to listen to and act upon, then it would not be subaltern.

Yet testimonio certainly has the effect of making subaltern experience and voice into something that "matters." In asking to "out" Stoll's questions about *I, Rigoberta Menchú* at the 1991 LASA conference, I wanted to address an issue that had been raised earlier (notably, by Elzbieta Sklodowska) in the discussion of testimonio in Latin American literary criticism: Was testimonio an authentic subaltern voice, or, to use one characterization, a "mediated" narrative in which a literary simulacrum of that voice was being staged, in the form of what Spivak called a "domesticated Other," for the reader, whose own position of relative authority and privilege was left uncontested in the process?

It turned out that the apparent coincidence between Stoll and myself was based on a misunderstanding on both our parts. Where Stoll was concerned with how testimonios like Menchú's got manipulated in the service of lethal Latin American political commissars or U.S.-style political correctness, I was concerned in my LASA talk with a different issue. Stoll's inability to grasp that issue is perhaps signaled when he remarks in his account that "the level of abstraction was beyond me." But my point was, in fact, not all that abstruse, although it was (and is) political in the deepest sense. It has to do with how people who are marginalized, repressed, and exploited, like Menchú at the time she told her story to Elisabeth Burgos in Paris, use something like testimonio for their purposes: that is, as a weapon, a way of fighting back. Because the key issue in testimonio, it seemed to me, was not, as both Stoll and Spivak made it, "representation." If the point of testimonio were simply to represent the subaltern *as subaltern,* victims as victims, then, as I note in "The Margin at the Center," it would be little more than a kind of postmodernist *costumbrismo,* the Spanish term for local-color writing. To recall Marx's well-known distinction, testimonio aspires not only to interpret the world but also to change it. Nevertheless, how one interprets the world also has to do with how one seeks, and is able, to change it. That idea—how testimonio might be understood as part of the agency of the subaltern—began to loom larger in the subsequent essays. Stoll and I went our separate ways.

It goes without saying that the event against which both Stoll's book and these essays must be weighed today is September 11, 2001, and its aftermath. Stoll and the neoconservative culture warriors who seized on his indictment of Menchú might seem to have the upper hand in this regard. Does September 11 mean the end of the political-ethical force of testimonio, with its demand for solidarity with the "wretched of the earth"? I believe that Stoll's polemic about *I, Rigoberta Menchú* belongs with the "red-baiting" approach to testimonio I mentioned earlier, in the sense that it is centered on the accusation that Menchú's narrative served as a propaganda vehicle for the Guatemalan armed struggle. But, for all practical purposes, that struggle was stalemated when *I, Rigoberta Menchú* first appeared in 1982, and was winding down by the time Stoll first made his charges against Menchú in 1990. *I, Rigoberta Menchú* is more likely to be read today in light of the concerns of feminism, post-colonialism, and multiculturalism than as a paean for armed struggle, and it is those concerns in particular that September 11 and the neoconservative ideological hegemony that resulted from it put into question.

But there is a hidden link between what were quintessentially "modern" forms of politics like armed national liberation struggles and the demands of identity politics and the new social movements today, which perhaps explains why Stoll himself shifts midway through his book from the question of advocacy of armed struggle in Guatemala to an attack on academic political correctness and what he calls "postmodernist anthropology" in the United States. It is true that the new social movements (which include an emergent indigenous Mayan movement in Guatemala, inspired in part by the figure and work of Menchú), unlike the guerrilla vanguards of the 1960s and 1970s, do not address the question of the conquest of state power. Like the Zapatistas in Mexico, their aim is more to create local and global circuits of consciousness-raising, resistance, and empowerment in civil society. But there is at least a moment in which, in the pursuit of their particularized or highly local demands, they must also begin to project alternative models of government, community, and economic life. That is the moment in which, individually or as a bloc, they must bid for, in Gramsci's phrase, "moral and intellectual leadership of the nation"—that is, hegemony. It seems to me that the continuing force of testimonio is linked to this moment—which is a political one—more than to the ethical-legal problematic of human rights that a writer such as Susan Sontag emphasizes (although it also needs to be said that the political and the ethical-legal dimensions of testimonio are not strictly separable). I continue to see in testimonio, in other words, a model for a new form of politics, which also means a new way of imagining the identity of the nation.

Acknowledgments

I would like to thank Jonathan Arac, Ofelia Schutte, and especially Amy Kaminsky for their helpful readings of the manuscript. Edward Said and Steve Sapolsky both contributed, in different ways, to these essays. This collection is dedicated to their memory.

Introduction
Testimony and Empire

Truth and Solidarity

"My name is Rigoberta Menchú. I am twenty-three years old. This is my testimony": the opening sentences of *I, Rigoberta Menchú*. "I'll begin by saying . . . ": the first words of Domitila Barrios de Chungara's testimonio about life in Bolivian mining communities. "Let me speak! Do not interrupt me! I have no time to listen to you. They are coming to take me at six o'clock this evening": the words of an Egyptian prostitute, Firdaus, about to be executed for killing her pimp to her interviewer, the feminist writer Nawal El Saadawi.[1] When we are addressed in this way, directly, as it were, even by someone who we would normally disregard, we are placed under an obligation to respond; we may act or not on that obligation, we may resent or welcome it, but we cannot ignore it. Something is asked of us by testimonio.

Is this voice reassuring or unsettling? On the whole, we would have to say reassuring, even in its expression of states of extreme desperation, suffering, and abjection. Reassuring because it has been produced *for us,* like a movie, by people like us (journalists, Amnesty International, editors, psychotherapists, academics, small feminist presses, Casa de las

Américas, ACT-UP . . .), and in a narrative form—the autobiography or bildungsroman—that is the form we would probably give the story of our own lives.

But this voice also comes to us from the place of an other, an other that is repressed or occluded by our own norms of cultural and class authority and identity. It has the force of what Freud called the uncanny (that sensation of uncanniness is part of the aesthetic effect of testimonio). It addresses us in the same way as the act of "hailing" in Althusser's account of ideology. But where in that account the enunciation of the policeman—"Hey, you there!"—interpellates us *as* subaltern (as always-already subject to the authority of the state), in testimonio we are in effect interpellated *from* the subaltern. So there are also moments in testimonio when we hear something that does not fit with our sense of political or ethical correctness. These moments summon us to a new kind of relationship with others, a new kind of politics.

In a justly famous essay, Richard Rorty distinguishes between what he calls the "desire of solidarity" and the "desire for objectivity":

> There are two principal ways in which reflective human beings try, by placing their lives in a larger context, to give sense to those lives. The first is by telling the story of their contribution to a community. This community may be the actual historical one in which they live, or another actual one, distant in time or place, or a quite imaginary one, consisting perhaps of a dozen heroes and heroines selected from history or fiction or both. The second way is to describe themselves as standing in an immediate relation to a non-human reality. This relation is immediate in the sense that it does not derive from a relation between such a reality and their tribe, or their nation, or their imagined band of comrades. I shall say that stories of the former kind exemplify the desire for solidarity, and that stories of the second kind exemplify the desire for objectivity.[2]

Is testimonio a form of the "desire for solidarity," then? That would certainly be a way of responding to someone like David Stoll, who takes testimonio to task for producing an illusion of facticity.[3] But that answer may be too easy, because the demand for solidarity that testimonio makes is founded on the assumption of its truth. It goes without saying that, as in any form of representation, what we encounter in testimonial narrative is not the Real as such, in Jacques Lacan's sense of "that which resists symbolization absolutely," but rather a "reality effect" created by the peculiar mechanisms and conventions of the text, which include a textual simulacrum of direct address. Nevertheless, it is what really happened, "the real thing," truth versus lie—the Big Lie of racism, imperialism, inequality, class rule, genocide, torture, oppression—that is at stake in testimonio.

That is why Doris Sommer's appeal to Wittgenstein's idea of language games in defense of Rigoberta Menchú's narrative strategy seems in some ways an insufficient response to Stoll.[4] The "conversation" we might have about testimonio as liberal intellectuals—Rorty's "self-reflective individuals"—in the upper reaches of the American academy is not the same thing as the sometimes life-and-death struggles that define testimonio's situation of enunciation, nor, for that matter, the situation of bitter ideological struggle that conditions how a text like *I, Rigoberta Menchú* is actually taught and read in classrooms in this country (one of the consequences of the fallout from Stoll's book has been its virtual disappearance from high school and college reading lists).

By the same token, it is not enough to allow, as Stoll in fact does, that testimonio can be valid as "literature" even where (in his view) it is not valid as history. The Mayan writer Victor Montejo responds:

> But if we know that the book [*I, Rigoberta Menchú*] has problems, how can we use it as a text? This is what David Stoll was asked during a conference in Berkeley at which I was a participant. Stoll said that he heard someone propose that the best way to teach it is to treat Menchú's biography as an epic novel. It is the truth, but mythologized, or call it a myth-history; we may treat the book as a collection of stories falling into the category of what Miguel Ángel Asturias called magical realism. I think this is a postmodern trick that will push back in time and make unreal the pain and suffering of the Mayans. Thus, it will be easy to forget that the reparation recommended by the truth commission has not yet been carried out. According to the epic approach, we can now read the Menchú book like *El poema de Mío Cid, Roldán*, or even the adventures of Don Quixote. To imagine the recent Guatemalan holocaust as an epic is to remove ourselves from the reality of this genocide that has left two hundred thousand deaths.[5]

The word *testimonio* in Spanish carries the connotation of an act of truth telling in a religious or legal sense—*dar testimonio* means to testify, to bear truthful witness. Testimonio's ethical and epistemological authority derives from the fact that we are meant to presume that its narrator is someone who has lived in his or her person, or indirectly through the experiences of friends, family, neighbors, or significant others, the events and experiences that he or she narrates. What gives form and meaning to those events, what makes them *history,* is the relation between the temporal sequence of those events and the sequence of the life of the narrator or narrators, articulated in the verbal structure of the testimonial text. A colleague at another university, Claudia Ferman, observes that in the wake of Stoll's book she was invited to talk about Menchú to a class. "After my presentation," she writes, "which addressed many aspects of Menchú's leadership, including the relevance of the Stoll controversy in terms of the U.S. academe and the battle over knowledge, I could not ignore some disappointment in my audience. After making inquiries, I came to realize that my talk did not address whether 'Menchú had lied or not,' which was central to the interest of that class."[6]

Central to the interest of any class, one might add. So let me be clear on this point: Menchú does not lie. Her account is not "myth." David Stoll does not accuse her of lying but of misrepresenting or eliding certain aspects of the story he thinks are crucial, which is something quite different from lying (I think that Stoll misrepresents the political situation in Guatemala that led people like Menchú to support armed struggle against a right-wing military dictatorship, but I don't think he lies about it). Those that do lie are the intellectuals in and out of the U.S. academy, such as David Horowitz, Dinesh D'Souza, or Daphne Patai, who, knowing this perfectly well, nevertheless use Stoll to argue that Menchú's testimonio is a "pack of lies" and that therefore it should not be taught in American schools or colleges. They lie consciously and deliberately, because they are concerned to discredit Menchú and what she represents, in the same way they were concerned to discredit the testimony of Anita Hill against Clarence Thomas. They lie because they believe that the end—hegemony of a neoconservative political and cultural agenda—justifies the means. They lie because they are part of what Hillary Clinton accurately characterized as "a vast right-wing conspiracy," a conspiracy that has given us, among other things, our present president and his administration.[7]

We are here in a situation of ideological struggle in which academic niceties about language games or "reality effect" are themselves liable to be negatively characterized as forms of political correctness. The reason Stoll was able to impeach Menchú's authority—in effect resubalternizing her—is that, like a good lawyer, he was able to pick holes in her story, giving the *appearance* that she was not completely reliable. In this sense, point-by-point refutations of the details of Stoll's charges, including those made by Menchú herself and her supporters, run the risk of ceding the ground of the debate to Stoll in the first place. That is because his deeper argument with testimonial narrative is not so much about the empirical details of what happened—the discrepancies he identifies in Menchú's account are, by his own admission, relatively minor and, in any case, subject themselves to further scrutiny and empirical verification—but rather over who has the authority to tell the story. Stoll's claim is that Menchú, by virtue of being an interested party to the events that she describes, cannot be objective, and the proof of her lack of objectivity are the absences or discrepancies he finds in her account, which, he feels, stem from the radical political agenda she is trying to promote.

This implies that there is an objective, value-free position distinct from that of the narrator, and that Stoll is in that position. But it is clear that Stoll, who describes himself as "a cautious social democrat,"[8] also has a political agenda: he thinks that the strategy of armed struggle pursued by the part of the Guatemalan left that Menchú identified with was a tragic error that provoked the genocidal counterinsurgency war by the army whose effects Menchú describes so vividly. His difference with Menchú, then, is not a difference between "solidarity" and "objectivity," but rather between two equally political—that is, equally ideological—positions, both of which are founded on a claim of truth.

That claim of truth makes Stoll's argument ideological in a second, specifically disciplinary or epistemological, sense. Stoll poses as a defender of the fact-gathering and evaluation procedures of anthropology and investigative journalism against what he characterizes as a "postmodernist" position that would grant authority to subaltern voice as such. That stance, which amounts to a reterritorialization of the disciplinary authority of anthropology, is founded on a vaguely Popperian, neopositivist notion of truth and verifiability that, outside the humanities, is still the dominant ideology of knowledge in most sectors of the American and global academy today. It is therefore a position that sits well with many academics and teachers, especially in the social and natural sciences, who may have felt threatened by the intrusion of critical theory into their once clearly delimited and policed domains. Like Alan Sokal in his celebrated hoax in the science wars, Stoll is playing to the crowd.

Where something like Sommer's appeal to Wittgenstein becomes both necessary and compelling, then, is in its recognition that the response to Stoll must involve not only arguments about facts but also an argument about what constitutes a fact. This is not a matter of denying the integrity or importance of scientific method or inquiry. Menchú herself is quite explicit on this point. She observes in an interview several years before the Stoll controversy broke: "I believe that Indians should take advantage and assimilate all those great values offered by the discoveries of science and technology. Science and technology have accomplished great things and we can't say 'we Indians aren't going to be part of that,' because in fact we are part of it."[9]

One of the most important aspects of the peace process in Guatemala, as in other countries that have passed through similar experiences of genocide, is the work of forensic anthropology in reconstructing the massacres committed by the army and paramilitary forces during the counterinsurgency war. What Menchú in her testimonio and a forensic scientist do in the reconstruction of a past obliterated by the violence of power are not alternative or antagonistic, but rather *complementary* projects, which in their own process of development create forms of dialogue, cooperation, and coalition between intellectuals, scientists, educators, artists, and social movements of the subaltern, crossing previous class, gender, and ethnic boundaries.[10] Those forms of cooperation and coalition can serve, in turn, as the basis for the articulation of a new historical bloc, at the level of both the nation-state and the global system. The society or societies such a bloc might bring into being would be one(s) in which science and culture would flourish in ways that are hard to imagine today. Testimonio in that sense is not the enemy of science; the enemies of testimonio are also the enemies of science.

Still, it is important to be aware of something that Menchú returns to again and again in her narrative: science, history, the law, literacy campaigns and formal education, literature, even the discourse of human rights itself (founded as it is on a liberal concept of self and interests) are not necessarily neutral or benevolent; they can sometimes be institutional practices and beliefs—constellated in or at the margins of the state and state ideological apparatuses—that *produce* the conditions of subalternity and repression that are represented in testimonio. Stoll thinks of himself as a person of the left. His aim in raising the kind of questions he does is to found the political goals and practice of the left on solid empirical and scientific foundations. To give up those foundations in the name of postmodernism, multicultural relativism, identity politics, "solidarity," and the like is, he feels, to give up the very weapon the left needs to use against capitalism.

But (it is an old question in Marxism), can one have a "left" politics with a "right" epistemology? The wide-ranging academic debate in the last decade or so over the nature and effects of testimonio as a narrative form that both Stoll's intervention and these essays are part of, by implicitly affirming the *sufficiency* of academic knowledge in relation to the phenomenon of testimonio, may serve, paradoxically, to distract us from recognizing that, while testimonio certainly seeks to address the academy, we are only *one* of the audiences it addresses, and not necessarily the most urgent or important one. In this sense, testimonio acts in the world as a regime of truth that operates "off campus," so to speak, like early Christianity outside the Temple and the Law.

I would suggest, then, that what testimonio requires of the academy is not that we "know" it adequately, but something like a critique of academic knowledge as such. That critique, which for us would amount to a kind of criticism/self-criticism, would point in the direction of relativizing the authority of academic knowledge—that is, *our* authority—but not to the rejection or abandonment of that knowledge. Rather, it would allow us to recognize what academic knowledge is in fact: not *the* truth, but *a form of* truth, among many others, that has fed processes of emancipation and enlightenment, but that is also both engendered and deformed by a tradition of service to the ruling classes and to institutional power.

To put this somewhat differently: what is at stake in testimonio is not so much truth *from* or *about* the other as the truth *of* the other. What I mean by this is the recognition not only that the other exists as something outside ourselves, not subject to our will or desires, but also of the other's sense of what is true and what is false.

Empire and Multitude

When we say that testimonio involves us in a relation of solidarity with the other, what exactly does that mean in terms of real or possible political consequences? And what does it mean, in particular, to ask that question after September 11? If Michael Hardt and Antonio Negri are right, and globalization portends something like a new Roman Empire in which there is no longer a center or periphery (for the Empire has no outside), then that question might be rephrased: Who are the Christians today? That is, who in the world today, within Empire but not *of* it, carries the possibility of a logic that is opposed to Empire and that will bring about its eventual downfall or transformation?

Even for those who continue to consider themselves Marxists in some sense, it no longer seems enough to say that this is the proletariat or the working class. Hardt and Negri themselves prefer the idea or image of the "multitude"—which they derive from Spinoza via the Italian political philosopher Paolo Virno.[11] My inclination would be to conflate their idea of the multitude with that of the subaltern, the "poor in spirit" in the words of the Sermon on the Mount. This would have the effect of opening up the category of the subaltern to the future, instead of seeing it (as Gramsci did, for example) as an identity shaped by the resistance of tradition to modernity.[12]

But there is a perhaps crucial difference between the multitude and the subaltern: the multitude, as Hardt and Negri use the term, is meant to designate a faceless or many-faced, hydra-headed, collective subject conjured up by globalization and cultural deterritorialization, whereas the subaltern is in the first place a specific identity as such, "whether this is expressed in terms of class, caste, age, gender and office or in any other way," to recall Ranajit Guha's definition.[13] It follows that the politics of the subaltern must be, at least in some measure, "identity" politics. In turn, if testimonio is both a representation and a form of agency of such a politics, then it is, or could be, the narrative form of what Hardt and Negri call the multitude, in the same way—and because of the same claim to the authority of direct witness—that the Gospels were the narrative form of early Christianity.

The problem here is that Hardt and Negri themselves go to some pains in *Empire* to argue that identity politics as they understand it (that is, as what usually is called "liberal multiculturalism") is itself deeply complicit with Empire. For if supra- or subnational permeability is the central economic characteristic of the new global capitalism, then multicultural heterogeneity is syntonic with this permeability in some ways, exploding or reordering at the level of the ideological superstructure previously hegemonic narratives of the unified nation-state and the people (*one* language, history, territoriality, etc.).

For Machiavelli, who was the first modern thinker of national liberation struggle, "the people" *(popolo)* is the condition for the nation and, in turn, realizes itself as a collective subject in the nation. What Hardt and Negri's concept of the multitude implies is that you can have "the people" without the nation. Machiavelli believed that "the people" without the nation is irremediably heterogeneous and servile—like the Jews in Egyptian captivity. It is the Prince—Moses—who confers on "the people" a unity of will and identity by making it into a nation. But the appeal to the idea of the nation also stabilizes that will and identity—as, now, *a* people—around a hegemonic vision, codified in the Law and the state apparatus, of a common language (or languages), set of values, culture, interests, community, tasks, sacrifices, historical destiny—a vision that rhetorically sutures over the gaps and discontinuities internal to "the people." But it is in those gaps and discontinuities that the force of the subaltern appears.

Seeming to mark a coincidence between the idea of the subaltern as a "radical heterogeneity" (Dipesh Chakrabarty's phrase) in excess of the nation-state and the concept of the multitude, Hardt notes, apropos

Rousseau, the limits of representative democracy and a unitary idea of "the people" as the subject of democracy:

> On the one hand, the people of a republic, [Rousseau] claims, must be absolutely sovereign and all must participate in an active and unmediated way in founding and legislating political society. . . . And yet on closer inspection we can see that, Rousseau's insistence to the contrary, his notion of sovereignty too contains a strong conception of representation. This is most clear in Rousseau's explanation that only the "general will" of the people is sovereign, not the "will of all." The general will itself is a representation that is simultaneously connected to and separate from the will of all. This corresponds to Rousseau's distinction between the people and the multitude. The people is only sovereign for Rousseau when it is unified. . . . The unity of the people is created through an operation of representation that separates it from the multitude. Despite the fact that the people all meet in person to exercise sovereignty, then, the multitude is not present; it is merely represented by the people. The rule of all is thus paradoxically but nevertheless necessarily reduced to the rule of one.[14]

Is the transcendence of the nation-state by globalization, assuming it to be the case (and I don't), fortuitous for the project of human emancipation and diversity, then? Hardt and Negri, following a tradition of Marxist antinationalism that goes back to Rosa Luxemburg, seem to think that it is. Their argument against multiculturalism in *Empire* is related to their argument against hegemony in Gramsci's sense of "moral and intellectual leadership of the nation." They want to imagine a form of politics that would go beyond the limits of both the nation and the forms of political and cultural representation traditionally bound up with the idea of hegemony—a politics of "absolute democracy," as they call it, after Spinoza. Thus, for example:

> The multitude is self-organization. Certainly, there must be a moment when reappropriation and self-organization reach a threshold and configure a real event. This is when the political is really affirmed—when the genesis is complete and self-valorization, the cooperative convergence of subjects, and the proletarian management of production become a constitutent power. This is the point when the modern republic ceases to exist and the postmodernist posse arises. This is the founding moment of an earthly city that is strong and distinct from any divine city. The capacity to construct places, temporalities, migrations, and

new bodies already affirms its hegemony through the actions of the multitude against the Empire. (*Empire*, 411)

But where would this "capacity to construct places, temporalities, migrations, and new bodies" come from if not from subjectivities defined by (subaltern) "identity"? *Empire* seems to move at times into a post-political register altogether, which depends paradoxically, in the fashion of Marx and Engels's "all that is solid melts into air," on the radicalizing power of capital itself, seen as the outcome of collective labor, to both transform and transnationalize the proletariat, in the process bursting apart the integument of the nation-state and allowing for the emergence of new forms of political activity and mobilization. One of these new forms, Hardt and Negri argue, appears around the question of the population displacements produced by globalization. Mass immigration, they claim, reveals the antagonism of the multitude—the subject both engendered by and opposed to global capital—and the anachronistic system of national borders. From this it follows that the "ultimate demand" of the multitude should be a demand for global citizenship.

This is certainly a legitimate demand, as is their related demand for a universal social wage. It is hard, though, to see it as a demand—even what Trotskyists call a "transitional demand" (a demand for a reform that if met would produce a chain of progressively more radical demands)—that would explode the limits of global capital or its emerging political-ideological superstructure; rather, it seems that global capital is the precondition for both making and fulfilling that demand. For Hardt and Negri, the multitude is an "expanded" way of naming the proletariat that does not limit it to the category of productive wage labor, a way of seeing the proletariat instead as a hybrid or heterogeneous subject conjured up by, but always already in excess of, capitalism at its present stage. We know, of course, that the idea of the subaltern played a similar role for Gramsci in the *Prison Notebooks,* beyond its usefulness as a euphemism to placate the prison censors. But how much of the radical potential of the multitude is at least in part a resistance to coming under formal or real subsumption in capitalist relations of production, that is, to becoming proletarianized? Isn't the distance or incommensurability between the "proletariat" (as defined by formal or real subsumption in capitalist relations of production) and the multitude—that is, between abstract and real labor—a difference marked precisely by, or as, "identity"? If this is so, then the question of multiculturalism and "identity" moves from the status of a secondary contradiction to become the, or a, main contradiction.

Hardt and Negri seem to approximate a recognition of the crucial role of identity, or, as they put it, "singularity," when they write:

> The multitude affirms its singularity by inverting the ideological illusion that all humans on the global surfaces of the world market are interchangeable. Standing the ideology of the market on its feet, the multitude promotes through its labor the biopolitical singularizations of groups and sets of humanity, across each and every node of global exchange. (395)

But there is an ambiguity here. Is it that they are noting the emergence of new logics of the social that oppose or resist the homogenizing effects of market capitalism in the name of (previously constituted?) "singularities," which now acquire in the face of capital a force of radical negativity? Or is the generalization of and abstraction of labor power produced by the commodification of human labor the precondition for "biopolitical singularizations of groups"? In the second case, the argument, though it appears in a postmodernist guise, is essentially similar to that of orthodox Marxism (to be specific, it resembles in some ways Karl Kautsky's idea of superimperialism). To be against capitalism, one must first have to be transformed by it. There can be no resistance to *becoming* proletarianized, only resistance from the position of being already subject to capital. Thus, "the telos of the multitude must live and organize its political space against Empire and within the 'maturity of the times' and the ontological conditions that Empire presents" (407). But, this is to subordinate the struggle against capital to the time of capital. If what the multitude resists is the "interchangeability" that results from the general commodification of labor and nature, then what it affirms as singularity are forms of cultural and psychic difference, time, need, and desire that are at odds with the "ontological conditions that Empire presents."

Hardt and Negri borrow Virno's metaphor of "Exodus" to describe the detachment of the multitude from the nation-state, envisioning a movement from the "modern republic" to the "postmodernist posse." But an Exodus to where? (Because Exodus is also for Virno "the foundation of a Republic.")[15] If their demand for global citizenship has a slightly reformist air, there is a more militant antagonism to Empire that is revealed in spontaneous and punctual acts of insurgency, which Hardt and Negri call forms of "constituent power," such as the Los Angeles riots after the Rodney King incident, the Zapatista rebellion in Chiapas, Seattle and the subsequent demonstrations against the World Trade Organization, or the Intifada. Christians versus Rome, in other words. Yet all of these events are deeply embedded in one form or other of identity politics.

Early Christianity was an ideology—indeed, it served Althusser as the very model of ideology. As such, it had to create new kinds of territoriality within the Empire (I understand territoriality to designate the relation between personal identity and space). What were the territorialities it created? Initially, the scattered "communities" of believers represented in the Epistles (Romans, Corinthians, Philippians, Ephesians . . .), but eventually, out of those communities, and with the breakdown of the Empire (a breakdown in part owing to their proliferation), nations, or at least the basis for the modern European nation-states.

If we put the question of multiculturalism and the question of the limits of the nation together, it becomes apparent that without the capacity to interpellate hegemonically the nation (which could be either an actual or a *possible* nation), identity politics has no other option than to be part of "the cultural logic of late capitalism" (to recall Jameson's phrase), because it simply expresses what is already the case—indeed, even desirable—within the rules of the game of the world market system and liberal democracy, rather than something that is driven to contravene those rules. Its radical potential as a site for mobilization against the power and hegemony of global capital therefore depends on the nation. Outside that territoriality it becomes what Coco Fusco calls "happy multiculturalism"—that is, an aspect of the ideological superstructure of globalized capital itself.

But the same criticism could be made of the idea of the multitude. If it cannot address itself to an instance of hegemony, that is, to "representation," is the action of the multitude political at all, or simply a kind of turbulence created and tolerated by the generalization of market relations (in the same way, as we learn from *The Matrix Reloaded,* that the rebel bands are themselves part of the logic of the Matrix, its way of self-correcting itself)? Might the idea of free-market choice in neoliberalism be a better ideological expression of the multitude's reality than communism or socialism? An earlier Marxism in Latin America supposed that the "indian question" would be solved through the proletarianization and acculturation of the indigenous peoples of the continent. José Carlos Mariátegui was one of the first to argue against this conception in the 1920s, noting that the bases for socialism could also be found in both pre-Columbian and contemporary features of precapitalist indigenous Andean societies. *I, Rigoberta Menchú* similarly forces us to recognize that the participation of indigenous groups in the armed struggle in Guatemala was directed in part against, or to limit, both their proletarianization and their acculturation/transculturation. Ideologically, therefore, that struggle required an affirmation of indigenous "identity": values, languages, customs, dress, and territoriality (especially crucial in this regard is the defense of communal land rights). It was not only an economic and political struggle, in other words, it was also an epistemological one. By contrast, the central assumption of Stoll's critique of Menchú is that indians, like anyone else, are essentially individualized market subjects, who operate according to a rational-choice paradigm of agency.

Hardt and Negri include indigenous struggles such as those represented in *I, Rigoberta Menchú* in their concept of the multitude. But the question remains: Are what they understand by ideological dynamics of the multitude the same thing as the ideological dynamics that actually motivate these struggles? Or have they subsumed those dynamics in their concept of the multitude, which risks becoming, like the orthodox Marxist concept of the proletariat, another "universal" subject?

The Nation and Modernity

There has been some effort to revive Leninism lately, most prominently (not to say hysterically) perhaps by Slavoj Žižek. But the crucial aspect of Lenin's thought that deserves continued attention in relation to our concerns here, in my opinion, is precisely one that someone like Žižek, who exhibits the same combination of "right" epistemology and "left" politics as Stoll and who shares with Stoll and Hardt and Negri a strong antipathy to identity politics, would not approve of. That is because it has to do with what was called in classical Marxism the "national question," which is, of course, at heart a question of national "identity."

To recall briefly Lenin's argument about the national question: In the stage of monopoly capitalism, based on competition for markets and raw materials and labor supply between national capitalisms, the main contradiction shifts from the capital–labor contradiction within the territoriality of given nation-states to the conflict between dominated and dominant nations or national groups. The main form of struggle in turn shifts from class-based unions and parties—the organizations of the Second International—to national liberation struggles, preferably "led" by the working class, but not limited to working-class interests as such. The locus of struggle similarly shifts from the advanced capitalist states of Western Europe and the United States to Asia, Africa, and Latin America.

It could be argued that underlying the conflict between the so-called free world and communism in the Cold War was a deeper conflict between forces of globalizing capitalism, based in, but no longer strictly limited to, the nation-state, and ethnic nationalisms located in what came to be called the Third World. If that is true, then the political and strategic contradiction between capitalism and communism consisted in the fact that communism acted as essentially a proxy and support for nationalism. A case could be made similarly that the problem of the nation and of national identity is still at the heart of global conflict, even though the nature of that conflict has shifted in the last quarter century. It is perhaps best to respond to the claim underlying *Empire* that the nation-form has been, or is in the process of being, transcended by the present stage of capitalism, which no longer requires that form in the way monopoly capital did (in that competition between respective national capitals was also military competition between nation-states): it is too early to tell. It may be that the partial disabling of the economic autonomy of the nation-state by globalization and the sometimes disastrous consequences this produces (for example, the collapse of Argentina's economy) may in some ways lend a new intensity and urgency to the national or the "local." Lenin and the Bolsheviks were attentive (it was their key point of difference with the Mensheviks) to the idea expressed in Trotsky's theory of combined and uneven development that the spread of capitalism did not always produce predictable effects of modernization. By contrast, as I noted earlier, Hardt and Negri's idea of Empire resembles nothing so much as Kautksy's theory of "superimperialism": that is, that the transnationalization of capital itself created a higher form of economic rationality that in turn would be the precondition of a properly socialist internationalism. One of the fault lines of combined and uneven development, then (and, in Lenin's view, the main fault line), was the nation.

Lenin's argument about the national question represents his most original and politically charged contribution to Marxist theory, in the sense that it introduced the possibility of a specifically "cultural" determination, at the same time locating that determination within the parameters of the Marxist analysis of capitalism as a dynamic system, through the concept of imperialism as a stage of capitalism with special characteristics. But the question of the nation today—that is, as a question not only about what nations have been but also about what they might become—is connected to multiculturalism and identity politics in a way that Leninism is not useful for understanding. That is because of a crucial epistemological failure in Lenin's conceptualization of the nation. The Russian empire was, in Lenin's image, the prison house of nations. While differing radically with Kautsky and the dominant tendencies in European social democracy on the question of imperialism and war, in thinking about what constituted a nation, however, Lenin (and thence Stalin in his 1914 essay on the national question) took over from Kautsky the idea that a nation was a permanent and relatively homogeneous community of language, territory, market, economy, psychology, and culture.

Soviet nationalities policy followed more or less this conception, aiming at a "union" of nominally independent republics, each built around a single dominant national or ethnic group, despite evident incoherences (what to do about Soviet Jews, for example, who were a people without a specific territoriality?) and adjustments dictated by Stalinist realpolitik (deportation or relocation of ethnic groups deemed hostile to the Soviet project, or settlement of Russian minorities in other "nations," like the Baltic republics). The notion of the nation itself as "multinational"—that is, multicultural—was rejected by Lenin and the Bolsehviks, including Trotsky, as "reformist." One can see the seeds of the breakup of both the Soviet Union and Yugoslavia—which both showed a tendency to fracture precisely along the "national" lines affirmed in the constitution of the various republics—in this conception.

The alternative position in early-twentieth-century Marxism on the national question was that of the Austro-Marxist Otto Bauer in his 1907 treatise *The Question of Nationalities and Social Democracy* (Lenin commissioned Stalin to write his essay on the national question in response to Bauer). Reflecting the multilinguistic and multiethnic character of the Austro-Hungarian Empire, then in decay, Bauer was concerned with the problem of minorities that, like the Russian Jews, possessed attributes of nationhood—what Bauer called a "community of will"—but not an independent territorial state founded on those attributes. Bauer set up the following problematic in this regard:

1. National or ethnic identities—"communities of will"—are not simply ideological hallucinations or forms of false consciousness, as the antinationalist position in Marxism and anarchism argued, but are themselves the determinate products of the impact of capitalist combined and uneven development on different populations. They involve what could be characterized as a contradiction between (national-ethnic) gemeinschaft and (capitalist-modern) gesellschaft.

2. In a liberal-democratic state, national or ethnic multiculturalism may be tolerated in principle, but in practice is always limited by the hegemony of a dominant nation or ethnic group.

3. Therefore, the same principle of self-determination that legitimizes the existing nation-state and the hegemony of the dominant national or ethnic group may then be used by disaffected minorities to demand states where they would be a majority.

4. Should these disaffected minorities then be allowed to become states? Can they, in any case, become states if they are territorially noncontiguous?

Bauer's response was to divorce the "community of will" of language, group experience, and psychology or "national character" from a territoriality defined explicitly as "national" in the conventional sense reflected in the Kautsky–Lenin position (that is, exhibiting a community of language, market, etc.), by imagining democratically organized forms of relative national autonomy and self-determination for national or ethnic minorities within a larger territoriality, which, however, would also be a nation in some sense or other, or, to use his own term, a "multinational state." As the editor of a recent reedition of Bauer's treatise in English remarks, Bauer challenges, in effect, the main assumptions of the contemporary world of nation-states: to wit, "that sovereignty is unitary and indivisible, that national self-determination requires the constitution of separate nation-states, and that nation-states are the only recognized international players."[16]

There is much that seems dated in Bauer's argument today. But there is also a basic impulse that is worth reconsidering, especially in a world marked by mass immigration and/or articulation of national boundaries over previous territorialities, national or otherwise (as the Chicana writer Gloria Anzaldúa puts it, "we didn't cross the border, the border crossed over us"; just as the Basques are a "community of will" within present-day Spain and France, there are non-Basques within what would become the Basque "nation"). One might see Bauer in this regard as the first theoretician of multiculturalism rather than cultural-linguistic-legal homogeneity as the basis for the identity of the nation. This makes him also one of the first Marxists after Marx to think outside the framework of a normative modernity.

That is an important achievement, because in many ways the argument between capitalism and socialism that framed the Cold War was essentially an argument about which of the two systems could best carry forward the possibility of a political, scientific, cultural, economic modernity latent in capitalism itself. The basic premise of Marxism as a modernizing ideology was that bourgeois society could not complete its own promise of emancipation and material well-being, given the contradictions inherent in the capitalist mode of production, contradictions above all between the social character of the forces of production and the private character of ownership and capital accumulation. Freeing the forces of production from the fetters of capitalist relations of production—so the familiar argument went—the state-socialist or quasi-socialist regimes inspired by the Soviet model would soon overcome these limitations, inaugurating an era of unprecedented economic growth, which in turn would be the material precondition for socialism and eventually the transition to communism. The—at least for our time—ultimately triumphant response of capitalism was that the force of the free market would be more dynamic and efficient in the long run in producing modernity and economic growth.

What was not in question on either side of this argument, however, was the desirability of modernity as such. In turn, the various forms of nationalism and national liberation struggle in the twentieth century shared this consensus (that is why, for example, dependency theory, with its idea of national economic "underdevelopment" caused by the unequal relations of the national economies of peripheral states to the core states of the capitalist center, became the underlying political economy of nationalism). Jürgen Habermas's concept of communicative rationality expresses the prospect of a society that is, or that could become, transparent to itself. As Bauer realized almost a century earlier, though, what opposes transparency or the universalization of communicative rationality is not only the conflict of tradition and modernity—that is, the "incompleteness" of modernity, to borrow Habermas's own phrase—but also the intensification of forms of social heterogeneity and difference produced in part by the very process of capitalist modernity itself. Bauer's problem was to imagine the project of the left as detached from the telos of modernity, particularly as it is incarnated in the "history" of the nation-state. (Trotsky's theory of combined and uneven development points in a similar direction, but does not break with a normative idea of modernity and economic modernization, by contrast.)

What is at stake here is the relationship between subalternity, narrative history, and the time of capital. Dipesh Chakrabarty formulates the problem in the following way:

> [S]ubaltern histories written with an eye to difference cannot constitute yet another attempt, in the long and universalistic tradition of "socialist" histories, to help erect the subaltern as the subject of modern democracies, that is, to expand the history of the modern in such a way as to make it more representative of society as a whole. . . . Stories about how this or that group in Asia, Africa, or Latin America resisted the "penetration" of capitalism do not, in this sense, constitute "subaltern" history, for these narratives are predicated on imagining a space that is external to capital—the chronologically "before" of capital—but that is at the same time a part of a historicist, unitary time frame within which both the "before" and "after" of capitalist production can unfold. The "outside" I am thinking of is different from what is simply imagined as "before or after capital" in historicist prose. This "outside" I think

of, following Derrida, as something attached to the category "capital" itself, something that straddles a border zone of temporality, that conforms to the temporal code within which "capital" comes into being even as it violates that code, something we are able to see only because we can think/theorize capital, but that also always reminds us that other temporalities, other forms of worlding, coexist and are possible. . . . Subaltern studies, as I think of it, can only situate itself theoretically at the juncture where we give up neither Marx nor "difference," for, as I have said, the resistance it speaks of is something that can happen only *within* the time horizon of capital and yet has to be thought of as something that disrupts the unity of that time. Unconcealing the tension between real and abstract labor ensures that capital/commodity has heterogeneities and incommensurabilities inscribed in its core.[17]

The equation between the nation-state and the modern rests on the fact that the problem of the state is to incorporate its population into its own modernity. The population—or sectors of the population—"lags behind" modernity (expressed as instrumental or bureaucratic reason). What the concept of ungovernability expresses is the incommensurability between the "radical heterogeneity" of the subaltern and the reason of state. Ungovernability—the quality of resistance or persistence that is expressed in testimonial voice—is the space of resentment, recalcitrance, disobedience, marginality, insurgency. But ungovernability also designates the failure of formal politics and of the nation—that is, of hegemony. In this sense, like Hardt and Negri's multitude or Giorgio Agamben's *homo sacer,* the subject that speaks in testimonio has a differential relation with the nation and the "general will" expressed in representative democracy: it is what is not, or not yet, the nation. It "interrupts" the "modern" narrative of the transition from feudalism to capitalism, the formation and consolidation of the nation-state, and the teleological passage through the different stages of capitalism (merchant, competitive, monopoly, imperialist, now global).

The privileging in postmodernist social theory of the concept of civil society might be seen as connected to the argument that testimonio is a new form of truth, since it is founded on a disillusion with the capacity of the state to organize society and to produce modernity in either a capitalist or a socialist form. But it would be a mistake to assume that the subaltern is necessarily coextensive with civil society. That is because the idea of civil society in its usual sense (Hegel's *bürgerliche Gesellschaft*) is also tied, like the state, to a narrative of "development" or "unfolding" *(Entwicklung),* which by virtue of its own requirements (formal education, literacy and scientific and technical education, nuclear family units, party politics, business, private property) excludes significant sectors of the population from full citizenship or limits their access to citizenship. That exclusion or limitation is what constitutes the subaltern.

It follows that what Chakrabarty calls the "politics of despair" of the subaltern may be driven by a resistance to or skepticism not only about the official nation-state but also about what constitutes civil society. The equation between civil society, culture, and hegemony in Gramsci and other thinkers of modernity runs up against the problem that subaltern negativity is often directed precisely against what is understood and valued as "culture" by dominant groups. That is why narrative texts like *I, Rigoberta Menchú* cannot be adequately contained within the category of "literature" without putting the category itself into crisis; in its staging of voice, testimonio affirms the authority of oral culture against processes of cultural modernization and transculturation that privilege literacy and written literature as norms of expression. Almost by definition, the voice that speaks in testimonio is *not*, in its act of enunciation, part of what Hegel would have understood as civil society or what Habermas means by the "public sphere": if it were, it would address us instead in novels, essays, films, TV shows, letters to the editor, op-ed pieces. On the other hand, testimonio as an *énoncé*—that is, as something materialized in the form of a transcript or text—serves to bring subaltern voice and experience into civil society and the public sphere. If testimonio comes, like Antigone's lament, from outside the limits of the state, it is also implicated in tracing the frontiers of the authority of the state and expanding the compass of what counts as expression in civil society. Testimonio lies outside the institutions of both literature and a "reading public," but it is necessarily directed to them in what seems like a remedial or restitutive act (hence, the trope that usually accompanies testimonio: the voice of the voiceless).

What is the relation between testimonio and hegemony, then? Gramsci's concept of hegemony corresponds to a stage of modernity in which citizenship and cultural authority cannot be separated from formal education and literacy, since the values and information required to exercise citizenship are available only, or primarily, through print media (that is why, for example, he saw the production of popular serial novels such as existed in nineteenth-century England or France as a necessary condition for the emergence of an Italian national-popular culture). With the advent of mass audiovisual culture, however, the masses make the transition from the primary orality of precapitalist peasant or rural culture to what the Brazilian writer Antonio Cándido called, despairingly, the "urban folklore" of the media, detouring around, so to speak, print culture and its special requirements and pleasures. Testimonio comes from the oral world of the "poor," but it is still part of what Ángel Rama called the "lettered city" in Latin America: the equation of the mastery of writing and books with power. This raises the question of mass popular culture, as it is apprehended by cultural studies, as an alternative to testimonio as the mode of expression of the multitude or the multitude-as-subaltern. Cultural studies is founded on the assumption that contemporary societies confront the problem that the narratives—including the canons of national literatures—that legitimize and organize the nation-state no longer coincide with the multiple logics of civil society. In fact, it is the crisis or sense of inadequacy of the nation-state provoked by globalization and transnationalized audiovisual culture that allows the category of civil society to appear in its full light: that is, as what Néstor García Canclini calls "interpretive communities of consumers," partially detached from a national referent (since the circulation of cultural goods has become supra- and subnational at the same time).

This line of thought might seem at first sight to be a variation of Gramsci's point about the possible noncoincidence between "the people" and the nation (that noncoincidence, to repeat, is what the concept of the subaltern designates). But the crisis of the nation-state is also the crisis of the solution Gramsci sought to this problem: that is, the idea of national-popular hegemony. Hegemony itself is seen by cultural studies as founded on an outmoded distinction that links subalternity to *premodern* and hegemony to *modern* forms of culture. In contemporary societies, so the argument goes, the tradition/modernity binary dissolves, and thus along with it the dichotomy subalternity/hegemony.[18]

Hardt and Negri borrow from cultural studies the idea that the category that expresses the dynamic of popular culture is hybridity more than subalternity. If hybridization is coextensive with civil society, however, the binary that is not deconstructed by cultural studies is the one that is constitutive of this normative (as opposed to descriptive) sense of hybridity: that is, the state/civil society dichotomy itself, where civil society is seen as the place where hybridity appears, as against the monological and homogenizing narrative of the nation-state. Thus, in seeking "democratically" to displace hermeneutic authority from bourgeois high culture to popular reception and "crossovers," cultural studies ends up in some ways, like Hardt and Negri's idea of absolute democracy, legitimizing the market and globalization. The very cultural logic it represents points in the direction of assuming that hegemony is no longer a possibility, because there no longer exists a common cultural basis for forming the collective national-popular subject required to exercise hegemony. There are only deterritorialized identities or identities in the process of becoming deterritorialized.

Fredric Jameson explains magic realism as entailing the coexistence in a given social formation of temporalities and value systems corresponding to different modes of production that bleed through each other, in the manner of a palimpsest.[19] But the generalization of the time of capital that globalization entails tends instead toward a single, overarching temporality—that of the circulation of commodities and "the end of history"—in which other historicities continue to exist simply as elements of pastiche. For Jameson, postmodernist historicist pastiche or *mode rétro* is possible only because history has lost its power to represent the subject and the national-popular.

If there was explicit in the idea of the melting pot, or *mestizaje,* a teleological narrative of the adaptation of "the people" to the state (and vice versa), a similar (albeit often unacknowledged), but now post-national, teleology operates in the concept of hybridity/hybridization in cultural studies, because it designates a dialectical process—seen as both inevitable and providential—of the "overcoming" of antinomies that are rooted in the immediate cultural and historical past, including the "past" of high modernism itself. Despite its gestures to postmodernism, then, cultural studies simply transfers the dynamic of modernization from the sphere of modernist high culture and the state ideological apparatuses to mass culture, now seen as more capable of producing "cultural citizenship." In this sense, cultural studies does not break with the values of modernity and does not, in itself, point beyond the limits of neoliberal hegemony. The positivist epistemology claimed by Stoll, founded on the authority of a rather reductionist vision of scientific method and an individualistic, rational-choice model of agency, and the discourse of civil society and hybridity mobilized by cultural studies in response to the new "flows" of economic and cultural globalization are two sides of the same coin: forms of the rationality of a capitalist modernity in which "traditional" identities and value systems now seen as anachronistic should disappear or be sublated in a new "mix."

A Radical Multiculturalism

Echoing Hardt and Negri's dismissal of multiculturalism, Gayatri Spivak writes in her book on the impact of globalization on literary studies, *Death of a Discipline,* "Autobiography is easy here [in the representation of globality]—the collectors of testimonies are waiting with their tape recorders, but irrelevant. . . . Identity politics is neither smart nor good."[20]

A full page separates these two remarks in her text, but there is no doubt that they are linked. My debt to Spivak is everywhere evident in this collection (although she would claim that I have not read her carefully enough); but I find this double injunction in particular both mistaken (autobiography and testimonio are not the same thing) and condescending, and thus linked to the very forms of power and reification of thought she claims to be contesting in her work. More to the point, perhaps, the injunction betrays both an identity and politics: a neo-Arnoldian cosmopolitanism (the high-minded schoolmarm admonishing the vulgar multiculturalists in the back of the room). Would it not be more honest to start from the premise that *all* politics, including our own, is identity politics, so that the issue is not so much identity politics as such, but rather whose and what identity politics?

We return, then, to Chakrabarty's idea of the "radical heterogeneity" of the subaltern. Is the exteriority of the subaltern simply a function of its anachronism, as in the privileging of orality in testimonio, or does it represent a contradictory alterity within modernity—"something that conforms to the temporal code within which capital comes into being while violating that code at the same time": different logics of the social and different modes of experiencing and conceptualizing history and value within the time of capital and the territoriality of the nation-state? No one doubts that in an era of conservative Restoration such as our own, multicultural demands for "recognition" could lead to new, apartheid-like forms of territoriality tolerated, and in some cases even encouraged, by both local states and the international system. It was the intention of the racist state in South Africa in creating legally autonomous and "self-determined" tribal states—the Bantustans—to avoid by this means the prospect that the black and colored population of the country could form a political majority that could take over the state. Perhaps this is what Spivak has in mind in her caution against identity politics. Similarly, Luis Tapia critiques the "truncated multiculturalism" of the contemporary Bolivian state and state ideological apparatuses (official recognition of linguistic and cultural differences; education programs in indigenous languages; creation of positions for indigenous representatives in state institutions; etc.). Such a multiculturalism appears in a progressive and democratic guise as a kind of postmodernist substitute for a prior revolutionary nationalism, but it also preserves the hierarchies embedded in multicultural difference, Tapia argues. The state recognizes the subaltern as such, but not as an agent of change or transformation; rather, it seeks to incorporate subaltern difference into *its* "modern" logic of representation and deliberation, a logic that in turn both naturalizes colonial hierarchies and guarantees the reproduction of capitalist relations of production.[21] What is radical in multicultural demands, what makes them the crucial arena for the formation of what Hardt and Negri call "constituent power," is not so much the desire for "recognition" or a "space of one's own," but rather the way these demands propose to redefine the identity of both the nation and the international order: that is, they are radical to the extent that they seek to *universalize* their singularity. What they ask of the state is not "recognition" of their alterity, but rather that the state recognize itself as other: that is, as always-already multicultural. The key question in this respect is not "difference" but equality.

In Frantz Fanon's succinct definition, the nation-state is a "bourgeois contrivance," and we would do well not to overlook this. But it would be a form of essentialism to argue that the idea of the nation as such is limited to only one form of class rule, and it would be shortsighted to found a political alternative to globalization on the negation of "contradictions among the people" in nations or between nations. That negation would amount to a postmodernist equivalent of the now discredited argument that in national liberation struggles women, gays, workers, peasants, and ethnic or racial minorities have to suspend their specific demands in favor of national "unity" against a common enemy. What might be envisioned instead is a new kind of politics that interpellates "the people" as a historical bloc within the framework of existing or possible nations, but not as a unitary, "modern" subject—the subject of Rousseau's General Will, to recall Hardt's comments cited earlier— rather, in the fashion of Bauer's "communities of will," as internally fissured, heterogeneous, multiple. To put this another way, the unity and mutual reciprocity of the elements of "the people" depends (as the image of the Rainbow Coalition was meant to symbolize) on a recognition of sociocultural difference and incommensurability—an affirmation, that is, of "contradictions among the people." Socialism would be the egalitarian sociopolitical and economic form of this difference and incommensurability, without resolving them into a transcendent or unitary cultural or political logic.

To construct the politics of the multitude today, under conditions of globalization and in the face of the neoliberal critique and privatization of state functions, may therefore in some circumstances require a *relegitimization* of the nation-state. But, of course, such a relegitimization would also require, at the same time, new concepts of the nation, of national identity and interests, of citizenship and democracy, of the "national-popular," and of the forms of political assembly and deliberation, and, finally perhaps, of politics itself. Would a radical multiculturalism mean the end of the nation as such, or is it rather a question of "queering" the nation? Is the anxiety about multicultural heterogeneity and the "rule of all" the same as the anxiety expressed in the idea of homosexual panic: that is, an anxiety about something that is always-already the case?

If testimonio is an art of memory, it is an art directed not only toward the memorialization of the past but also to the constitution of more heterogeneous, diverse, egalitarian, and democratic nation-states, as well as forms of community, solidarity, and affinity that extend beyond or between nation-states. To construct such forms of community, however, it is necessary to begin with the recognition of an authority that is not our own, an authority that resides in the voice of others. In this sense, testimonio, despite its ambiguities and contradictions, continues to be part of a necessary pedagogy.

September 11

> No *"we"* should be taken for granted when the subject is looking at other people's pain.
>
> Susan Sontag, *Regarding the Pain of Others*

The September 11, 2001, terrorist attacks on the World Trade Center and the Pentagon seem to legitimize Samuel Huntington's idea of a "clash of civilizations" (the West versus the rest), and to oblige us, finally, to abandon sentimental Third Worldism and line up with our own kind, like Tony Blair. The casualties of September 11, then, may well include testimonio itself and multiculturalism. One of my students, a former Sandinista, remarked in the wake of the attacks: "This means the end of the utopian horizon of multiculturalism." But September 11 also meant that the American people have become, or become once again, a testimonial people; that is, we have had to come face to face as a people with the sense of catastrophe, unjustified massacre, irremediable loss, displacement, trauma, incomplete or inadequate mourning, and anger that marks the "situation of urgency" (to borrow René Jara's phrase) from which testimonio emerges. It is no accident in this sense that testimonial forms familiar from struggles against political repression and state violence in Latin America—enlarged, poster-size photos of the disappeared, for example—were one of the principal ways in which the anniversary of the attacks was commemorated. What is it, politically, that the use of these forms encourages, however?

The terrorist attack was directed against a homogeneous corporate-imperial America symbolized by the Pentagon and the World Trade Center, but its immediate aftermath revealed instead a "real" multicultural, middle- and working-class America among the victims. In the symbolic reading of the names of the dead on the anniversary of September 11—a common form of testimonial commemoration—a significant number were Hispanic. Many of them, we know, were illegal immigrants from countries like El Salvador or Guatemala, fleeing the counterrevolutionary violence described in testimonios like *I, Rigoberta Menchú* and working for minimum wage in the interstices of the new global cities.

But that recognition also poses a difficult question. Can we embrace, in the name of multiculturalism and subalternity, at the same time the victims of the terrorist attacks and the terrorists themselves? Are organizations like Al Qaeda and the larger movement of Islamic fundamentalism they grow out of forms of what Hardt and Negri mean by the multitude? It is no secret that the roots of Islamic fundamentalism lie in the conditions of poverty, inequality, frustration, lack of democracy, and hopelessness of masses of people in the Islamic world today, and that this situation, in turn, grows out of the defeat or perversion of socialist or nationalist projects of secular modernization. But it is also no secret that Osama bin Laden and his organization, as the direct creation of the collaboration between the Saudi monarchy, the military dictatorship in Pakistan, feudal clergy and landlords in Afghanistan and elsewhere, Israeli realpolitik, and the CIA, were also one of the instruments of the defeat or corruption of Arab socialism and secular nationalism. Both the Taliban and Al Qaeda have shown that they are explicitly opposed to anything like the idea of a democratic, diverse, multicultural, egalitarian society. In that sense, they are closer to other emerging authoritarian capitalist ideologies, like the neo-Confucianism of the new entrepreneurial elites in China and the Asian Tigers (it is no accident that the bin Laden family is one of the most powerful business groups in the Middle East). Huntington's "clash of civilizations" may be a more accurate picture of the state of the world today than Hardt and Negri's *Empire*; but it is, from the point of view of the subaltern and the oppressed, a conflict between two different forms of reactionary hegemony, both founded on the perpetuation of hierarchical, class- and gender-divided societies, and the concomitant use of military violence against civilian populations.

Yet there is something about the links between imperialism, fundamentalist terrorism, and oppression and poverty in the Islamic world that is not easily dealt with by the "blowback" argument. I am aware in particular that the invocation of the subaltern and "contradictions among the people" does not do justice to the problem of *intra subaltern* violence: alienated Arab young men, many of them from middle-class backgrounds, kill undocumented Guatemalan immigrants, some of whom might have been militants in or supporters of the revolutionary movement in their country in the 1980s. The examples can only too easily be multiplied: the genocidal conflict between Tutsis and Hutus in Rwanda; the violent civil war between Islamic fundamentalists and secular nationalists in Algeria that has been going on for almost a quarter century; the struggle between Catholic and Protestant working-class communities in Northern Ireland; the simmering resentment between African Americans and Latinos in American inner cities; the tension between mestizos and indians in many Latin American countries; the deep persistence of forms of racism and male chauvinism in many, perhaps all, subaltern groups.

It is not enough to say that these conflicts are the heritage of colonialism— of British "divide and rule," for example—although of course they are (Bush's war in Iraq is nothing less than a contemporary version of an English colonial war). The problem is built into identity politics itself, which by its very nature runs the risk of "ethnicizing" politics.

In a conference at Columbia University some years ago that brought together members of the South Asian and Latin American Subaltern Studies Groups, the African social scientist Mahmood Mamdani asked if, to avoid another case of genocidal ethnic war such as Rwanda, a "sub-lation" of ethnic identity rather than its affirmation as a site of loss and recrimination was not what one should be aiming for. In a similar vein, Aamir Mufti, developing a position long argued by Edward Said, has renewed a call for a "critical secularism" as a way of displacing religious fundamentalism as an articulating principle of politics in the Islamic world.[22]

These suggestions return us to the question of the limits of modernity. It goes without saying that something like what Mufti understands by critical secularism is my own ideology, in the sense that Althusser spoke about the "spontaneous ideologies" of intellectuals, and that I feel an ethical, intellectual, and political responsibility to defend it. Yet it is entirely possible that to produce the sort of secularized citizen-subject Mamdani or Mufti have in mind—someone (like ourselves, that is) who would not be drawn into genocidal conflicts over identity of the Tutsi–Hutu or Palestinian–Israeli sort—out of the immense variety of populations and groups in the world today would require a violence as great as, if not greater than, intra subaltern violence. Despite their appeal to common sense and decency, and the possibility they afford of long-run alternatives to the carnage house that is world politics today, such positions run the risk in the short run of lending themselves to legitimize the violence of the core states of the global order, especially the United States. It might be argued, conversely, that many instances of intra subaltern violence, like the massacres in Rwanda, have their roots precisely in previous efforts to control and manipulate populations in the name of secularization and modernization. Soviet policy in Afghanistan was enlightened in many ways (for example, in seeking to implement agrarian reform and to extend women's rights). Its failure, which presaged the collapse of the Soviet Union itself and which concretely gave rise to Al Qaeda and the Taliban, is exemplary of the failure not so much of the core values of secular modernity—equality, democracy, socialism—but of a certain way of coercively implementing those values from above through the state or mililtary intervention on populations that, often in the name of "tradition" or religious beliefs, are reticent to accept them.

Does that mean that reaction always wins, even among the "poor"? But if Afghanistan reveals the limits of Communism as a form of modernity, both the Taliban and the regime installed by the Anglo-European military occupation of that country are also clearly "failed states," as will be the neocolonial state that emerges from the military occupation of Iraq. None of these regimes represents or will conceivably represent anything like a genuinely democratic, multicultural, egalitarian society. None of them was or is a "people-state," in Gramsci's sense of that term. Yet all of them speak the language of modernity (or countermodernity).

One needs to ask in reply to Mamdani then: not only sublation to what but also sublation by whom? Testimonio is, to recall again a phrase from Ranajit Guha, the "small voice of history": that is, the voice of the subaltern. But it is not the intention of this voice simply to display its subalternity. It speaks to us as an "I" that nevertheless stands for a multitude. It affirms not only a singular experience of truth in the face of grand designs of power, but truth itself as singularity. The problem of the politics of testimonio may be seen in this sense as linked to the problem of democracy itself: how to produce a general will out of a multiplicity of individual or group wills? The trick would seem to be finding a commonality in singularity—which is what I think the relation between testimonial voice and interlocutor/reader in testimonio enacts—and using that commonality politically as the basis for a new historical bloc capable of taking on reactionary hegemony. To achieve real equality, real democracy, economic well-being, ecological balance, cultural diversity, and change will require dismantling that hegemony at the level of both the nation-state—and above all the United States—and the global system. That, of course, is something easier said than done. In relation to this prospect, however, the critique of identity politics evident in different ways in Stoll's critique of testimonio and Hardt and Negri's *Empire* seems in some ways more part of the problem than the solution. It is part of the problem not only because it disenables agency; it also disenables a clear and compelling vision of the kind of society we claim to stand for.

1
The Margin at the Center:
On Testimonio

The deformed Caliban—enslaved, robbed of his island, and trained to speak by Prospero—rebukes him thus: "You taught me language and my profit on'it / Is, I know how to curse."[1]

Do social struggles give rise to new forms of literature, or is it more a question of the adequacy of their representation in existing narrative forms such as the short story and the novel, as in, for example, Gayatri Spivak's articulations of the stories of the Bengali writer Mahasweta Devi or Fredric Jameson's notion of national allegory in Third World writing?[2] What happens when, as in the case of western Europe since the Renaissance, there has been a complicity between the rise of "literature" as a secular institution and the development of forms of colonial and imperialist oppression against which many of these struggles are directed? Are there experiences in the world today that would be betrayed or misrepresented by the forms of literature as we know it?

Raymond Williams formulates a similar question in relation to British working-class writing:

> Very few if any of us could write at all if certain forms were not available. And then we may be lucky, we may find forms which correspond

to our experience. But take the case of the nineteenth century working-class writers, who wanted to write about their working lives. The most popular form was the novel, but though they had marvelous material that could go into the novel very few of them managed to write good or any novels. Instead they wrote marvelous autobiographies. Why? Because the form coming down through the religious tradition was of a witness confessing the story of his life, or there was the defense speech at a trial when a man tells the judge who he is and what he had done, or of course other kinds of speech. These oral forms were more accessible forms centered on "I," on the single person. . . . The novel with its quite different narrative forms was virtually impenetrable to working-class writers for three or four generations, and there are still many problems in using the received forms for what is, in the end, very different material. Indeed the forms of working-class consciousness are bound to be different from the literary forms of another class, and it is a long struggle to find new and adequate forms.[3]

Let me set the frame of the discussion a bit differently than Williams does. In the period of what Marx describes as the primitive accumulation in western Europe—say 1400 to 1650, which is also the age of the formation of the great colonial empires—there appears or reappears, under the impetus of humanism, a series of literary forms: the essay; the short story or *novela ejemplar*; the picaresque novel; the various kinds of Petrarchan lyric, including the sonnet; the autobiography; and secular theater. These forms, as ideological practices, are also a *means* (in the sense that they contribute to the creation of the subject form of "European Man"). By the same token, then, we should expect an age such as our own—also one of transition or the potential for transition from one mode of production to another—to experience the emergence of new forms of cultural and literary expression that embody, in more or less thematically explicit and formally articulated ways, the social forces contending for power in the world today. I have in mind here, by analogy to the role of the bourgeoisie in the transition from feudalism to capitalism, not only the struggle of working people everywhere against exploitation, but also in contingent ways movements of ethnic or national liberation, the women's liberation movement, poor and oppressed peoples' organizations of all types, the gay rights movement, the peace movement, ecological activism, and the like. One of these new forms in embryo, I will argue, is the kind of narrative text that in Latin American Spanish has come to be called testimonio.

By testimonio I mean a novel or novella-length narrative in book or pamphlet (that is, printed as opposed to acoustic) form, told in the first person by a narrator who is also the real protagonist or witness of the events he or she recounts, and whose unit of narration is usually a "life" or a significant life experience. Testimonio may include, but is not subsumed under, any of the following textual categories, some of which are conventionally considered literature, others not: autobiography, autobiographical novel, oral history, memoir, confession, diary, interview, eyewitness report, life history, *novela-testimonio*, nonfiction novel, or "factographic" literature. I will deal in particular with the distinctions among testimonio, life history, autobiography, and the all-encompassing term "documentary fiction" suggested by Barbara Foley.[4] However, because testimonio is by nature a protean and demotic form not yet subject to legislation by a normative literary establishment, any attempt to specify a generic definition for it, as I do here, is at best provisional, and at worst repressive.

As Williams suggests, testimonio-like texts have existed for a long time at the margin of literature, representing in particular those subjects—the child, the "native," the woman, the insane, the criminal, the proletarian— excluded from authorized representation when it was a question of speaking and writing for themselves rather than being spoken for. But for practical purposes we can say that testimonio coalesced as a new narrative genre in the 1960s and further developed in close relation to the movements for national liberation and the generalized cultural radicalism of that decade. Testimonio is implicitly or explicitly a component of what Barbara Harlow has called "resistance literature."[5] In Latin America, where testimonio has enjoyed an especially rich development, it was sanctioned as a genre or mode by two related developments: the 1970 decision of Cuba's Casa de las Américas to begin awarding a prize in this category in its annual literary contest, and the reception in the late 1960s of Truman Capote's *In Cold Blood* (1965) and Miguel Barnet's *Autobiography of a Runaway Slave/Biografía de un cimarrón* (1967).[6]

But the roots of testimonio go back to the importance in previous Latin American literature of a series of nonfictional narrative texts, such as the colonial *crónicas* and the "national" essay *(Facundo, Os sertões)*, the war diaries *(diarios de campaña)* of, for example, Bolívar or Martí, or the Romantic biography, a key genre of Latin American liberalism. This tradition combined with the wide popularity of the sort of anthropological or sociological life history composed out of tape-recorded narratives developed by academic social scientists such as Oscar Lewis or Ricardo Pozas in the 1950s.[7] Testimonio also drew on—in my opinion, much more crucially—the sort of direct-participant account, usually presented without any literary or academic aspirations whatever (although often with political ones), represented by books such as Che Guevara's *Reminiscences of the Cuban Revolutionary War* (1959), one of the defining texts of 1960s leftist sensibility throughout the Americas. The success of Che's account (with its corresponding how-to manual, *Guerrilla Warfare*) inspired in Cuba a series of direct-participant testimonios by combatants in the July 26th Movement and later in the campaigns against the counterrevolutionary bands in the Escambray mountains and at the Bay of Pigs. In a related way (in some cases, directly), there begins to emerge throughout the Third World, and in very close connection to the spread of armed-struggle movements and the Vietnam War, a literature of personal witness and involvement designed to make the cause of these movements known to the outside world, to attract recruits, to reflect on successes or failures of the struggle, and so on.[8]

The Spanish word *testimonio* translates literally as "testimony," as in the act of testifying or bearing witness in a legal or religious sense. This connotation is important because it distinguishes testimonio from recorded participant narrative, as in the case of "oral history." In oral history it is the intentionality of the recorder—usually a social scientist—that is dominant, and the resulting text is in some sense "data." In testimonio, by contrast, it is the intentionality of the narrator that is paramount. The situation of narration in testimonio has to involve an urgency to communicate, a problem of repression, poverty, subalternity, imprisonment, struggle for survival, implicated in the act of narration itself. The position of the reader of testimonio is akin to that of a jury member in a courtroom. Unlike the novel, testimonio promises by definition to be primarily concerned with sincerity rather than literariness. This relates testimonio to the generic 1960s practice of "speaking bitterness," to use the term popularized in the Chinese Cultural Revolution, evident, for example, in the consciousness-raising sessions of the women's liberation movement, Fanon's theory of decolonization, the pedagogy of Paolo Freire (one of the richest sources of testimonial material has been in the interaction of intellectuals, peasants, and working people in literacy campaigns), and Laingian and, in a very different way, Lacanian psychotherapies. Testimonio, in other words, is an instance of the New Left and feminist slogan "The personal is political."[9]

Because in many cases the narrator is someone who is either functionally illiterate or, if literate, not a professional writer, the production of a testimonio generally involves the tape-recording and then the transcription and editing of an oral account by an interlocutor who is an intellectual, often a journalist or a writer. (To use the Russian formalist term, testimonio is a sort of *skaz,* a literary simulacrum of oral narrative.) The nature of the intervention of this gathering and editing function is one of the more hotly debated theoretical points in the discussion of the genre, and I will come back to it. What needs to be noted here is that the assumed lack of writing ability or skill on the part of the narrator of the testimonio, even in those cases where the story is written instead of narrated orally, also contributes to the "truth effect" the form generates.

The situation of narration in the testimonio suggests an affinity with the picaresque novel, particularly with that sense of the picaresque that sees the hero's act of telling his or her life as yet another picaresque act. But testimonio, even where it approximates in content a kind of neo-picaresque, as it does quite often, is a basically different narrative mode. It is not, to begin with, fiction. We are meant to experience both the speaker and the situations and events recounted as real. The "legal" connotation implicit in its convention implies a pledge of honesty on the part of the narrator that the listener/reader is bound to respect.[10]

Moreover, testimonio is concerned not so much with the life of a "problematic hero"—the term Georg Lukács uses to describe the nature of the hero of the bourgeois novel[11]—as with a problematic collective social situation in which the narrator lives. The situation of the narrator in testimonio is one that must be representative of a social class or group. In the picaresque novel, by contrast, a collective social predicament, such as unemployment and marginalization, is experienced and narrated as a personal destiny. The "I" that speaks to us in the picaresque or first-person novel is in general the mark of a difference, an antagonism to the community, the *Ich-form* (Hans Robert Jauss's term)[12] of the self-made man: hence the picaresque's cynicism about human nature, its rendering of lower-class types as comic, as opposed to the egalitarian reader–character relation implied by both the novel and testimonio. The narrator in testimonio, on the other hand, speaks for, or in the name of, a community or group, approximating in this way the symbolic function of the epic hero, without at the same time assuming the epic hero's hierarchical and patriarchal status. René Jara speaks of an "epicidad cotidiana," an everyday epicality, in testimonio.[13] Another way of putting this would be to define testimonio as a nonfictional, popular-democratic form of epic narrative.

By way of example, here is the opening of *I, Rigoberta Menchú,* a well-known testimonio by a Guatemalan Indian woman:

> My name is Rigoberta Menchú. I am twenty-three years old. This is
> my testimony. I didn't learn it from a book and I didn't learn it alone.
> I'd like to stress that it's not only *my* life, it's also the testimony of my

people. It's hard for me to remember everything that's happened to me in my life since there have been many very bad times but, yes, moments of joy as well. The important thing is that what has happened to me has happened to many other people too: My story is the story of all poor Guatemalans. My personal experience is the reality of a whole people.[14]

Rigoberta Menchú was and is an activist on behalf of her community, the Quiché-speaking indians of the western highlands of Guatemala, and so this statement of principles is perhaps a little more explicit than is usual in a testimonio. But the metonymic function of the narrative voice it declares is latent in the form, is part of its narrative convention, even in those cases when the narrator is, for example, a drug addict or criminal. Testimonio is a fundamentally democratic and egalitarian form of narrative in the sense that it implies that any life so narrated can have a kind of representational value. Each individual testimonio evokes an absent polyphony of other voices, other possible lives and experiences. Thus, one common formal variation on the classic first-person singular testimonio is the polyphonic testimonio, made up of accounts by different participants in the same event.

What testimonio does have in common with the picaresque and with autobiography, however, is the powerful textual affirmation of the speaking subject. This should be evident in the passage from *I, Rigoberta Menchú* quoted above. The dominant formal aspect of the testimonio is the voice that speaks to the reader in the form of an "I" that demands to be recognized, that wants or needs to stake a claim on our attention. This presence of the voice, which we are meant to experience as the voice of a real rather than a fictional person, is the mark of a desire not to be silenced or defeated, a desire to impose oneself on an institution of power, such as literature, from the position of the excluded or the marginal. Fredric Jameson has spoken of the way in which testimonio produces a "new anonymity," a form of selfhood distinct from the "overripe subjectivity" of the modernist bildungsroman.[15] But this way of thinking about testimonio runs the risk of conceding to the subjects of testimonio only the "facelessness" that is already theirs in the dominant culture. One should note rather the insistence on and affirmation of the individual subject evident in such titles as *I, Rigoberta Menchú* (even more strongly in the Spanish, *Me llamo Rigoberta Menchú y así me nació la conciencia*), *Juan the Chamula (Juan Peréz Jolote)*, *Let Me Speak! Testimony of Domitila, a Woman of the Bolivian Mines*, *Doris Tijerino: Inside the Nicaraguan Revolution ("Somos millones . . .": La vida de Doris María)*.[16] Rather than a "decentered" subjectivity, which, in what has

been called the "Koreanization" of the world economy, is almost synony-
mous with cheap labor, testimonio constitutes an affirmation of the individual self in a collective mode.[17]

In a related way, testimonio implies a challenge to the loss of the
authority of orality in the context of processes of cultural modernization
that privilege literacy and literature as norms of expression. It allows
the entry into literature of persons who would normally, in those societies where literature is a form of class privilege, be excluded from direct
literary expression, persons who have had to be "represented" by professional writers. There is a great difference between having someone like
Rigoberta Menchú tell the story of her people and having that story told,
however well, by someone like, say, the Nobel Prize-winning Guatemalan
novelist Miguel Ángel Asturias.[18]

Testimonio involves a sort of erasure of the function, and thus also
of the textual presence, of the "author," which by contrast is so central
in all major forms of bourgeois writing since the Renaissance, so much
so that our very notions of literature and the literary are bound up with
notions of the author, or, at least, of an authorial intention. In Miguel
Barnet's phrase, the author has been replaced in testimonio by the function of a "compiler" *(compilador)* or "activator" *(gestante),* somewhat
on the model of the film producer.[19] There seems implicit in this situation
both a challenge and an alternative to the patriarchal and elitist function
the author plays in class and sexually and racially divided societies: in
particular, a relief from the figure of the "great writer" or writer as cultural hero that is so much a part of the ideology of literary modernism.

The erasure of authorial presence in the testimonio, together with its
nonfictional character, makes possible a different kind of complicity—
might we call it fraternal/sororal?—between narrator and reader than is
possible in the novel, which, as Lukács has demonstrated, obligates an
ironic distancing on the part of both novelist and reader from the fate of
the protagonist. Eliana Rivero, writing about *La montaña es algo más que
una inmensa estepa verde,* a testimonio by the Sandinista guerrilla coman-
dante Omar Cabezas (published in English as *Fire from the Mountain*),[20]
notes that "the act of speaking faithfully recorded on the tape, transcribed
and then 'written' remains in the testimonio punctuated by a repeated
series of interlocutive and conversational markers . . . which constantly
put the reader on alert: 'True? Are you following me? OK? So . . .'" She
concludes that the testimonio is a "snail-like discourse *[discurso encaraco-
lado]* which turns on itself and which in the process totally deautomatizes
the reaction of the reader, whose complicity it invites through the medium
of his or her counterpart in the text, the direct interlocutor."[21]

Just as testimonio implies a new kind of relation between narrator and reader, the contradictions of sex, class, race, and age that frame the narrative's production can also reproduce themselves in the relation of the narrator to this direct interlocutor. This is especially so when, as in *I, Rigoberta Menchú,* the narrator is someone who requires an interlocutor with a different ethnic and class background in order first to elicit the oral account, then to give it textual form as a testimonio, and finally to see to its publication and distribution. (In cases where testimonios are more directly a part of political or social activism—for example, in the use of testimonio in liberation theology–based community dialogues or as a kind of cadre literature internal to leftist or nationalist groups—these editorial functions are often handled directly by the party or movement in question, constituting then not only a new literary form but also new, noncommodified forms of literary production and distribution.)

I do not want to minimize the nature of these contradictions; among other things, they represent the possibility for a depoliticized articulation of the testimonio as a sort of *costumbrismo* (the Spanish word for "local-color" writing) of the subaltern or for the smothering of a genuine popular voice by well-intentioned but repressive (Stalinist, feminist, humanist, and so on) notions of "political correctness" or pertinence. But there is another way of looking at them. It is a truism that successful revolutionary movements in the colonial and postcolonial world have generally involved a union of working-class—or, to use the more inclusive term, popular—forces with a radicalized intelligentsia, drawn partly from formally educated sections of the peasantry and working class but also from the petite bourgeoisie and déclassé bourgeois or oligarchic strata that have become imbued with socialist ideas, organizational forms, culture, and so on. (Lenin was among the first to theorize this phenomenon in *What Is to Be Done?*) In this context, the relation of narrator and compiler in the production of a testimonio can function as an ideological figure or image of the possibility of union of a radicalized intelligentsia and the poor and working classes of a country. To put this another way, testimonio gives voice in literature to a previously "voiceless," anonymous, collective popular-democratic subject, the *pueblo* or "people," but in such a way that the intellectual or professional, usually of bourgeois or petit bourgeois background, is interpellated as being part of, and dependent on, the "people" without at the same time losing his or her identity as an intellectual. In other words, testimonio is not a form of liberal guilt. It suggests as an appropriate ethical and political response more the possibility of solidarity than of charity.[22]

The audience for testimonio, either in the immediate national or local context or in metropolitan cultural centers, remains largely that reading public that in presocialist societies is still a partially gender- and class-limited social formation, even in the "advanced" capitalist democracies. The complicity a testimonio establishes with its readers involves their identification—by engaging their sense of ethics and justice—with a popular cause normally distant, not to say alien, from their immediate experience. Testimonio in this sense has been important in maintaining and developing the practice of international human rights and solidarity movements. It is also a way of putting on the agenda, within a given country, problems of poverty and oppression, for example, in rural areas that are not normally visible in the dominant forms of representation.

The compiler of Rigoberta Menchú's testimonio, Elisabeth Burgos-Debray, was a Venezuelan social scientist living in Paris at the time she met Menchú, with all that implies about contradictions between metropolis and periphery, high culture and low culture, dominant and emergent social formations, dominant and subaltern languages. Her account of the relationship she developed with Menchú in the course of doing the testimonio forms the preface to the book, constituting a sort of testimonio about the production of a testimonio. One of the problems the two women encountered is that Menchú had to speak to Burgos-Debray in Spanish, the language for her of the ladinos or mestizos who oppressed her people, which she had just and very imperfectly learned (the conflict in Guatemala between Spanish and indigenous languages is in fact one of the themes of her narrative). In preparing the text, Burgos-Debray had to decide, then, what to correct and what not to correct in Menchú's recorded speech. She left in, for example, repetitions and digressions that she considered characteristic of oral narrative. On the other hand, she notes that she decided "to correct the gender mistakes which inevitably occur when someone has just learned to speak a foreign language. It would have been artificial to leave them uncorrected and it would have made Rigoberta look 'picturesque', which is the last thing I wanted."[23]

One could speak here, in a way familiar from the dialectic of master and slave or colonizer and colonized, of the interlocutor manipulating or exploiting the material the informant provides to suit her own cosmopolitan political, intellectual, and aesthetic predilections. K. Millet makes the following argument, for example, about the testimonio of an indigenous woman, *Los sueños de Lucinda Nahuelhual,* compiled by the Chilean feminist activist Sonia Montecino Aguirre:

> *Los sueños de Lucinda Nahuelhual* is not a narrative about a Mapuche Indian woman, but rather it is a textualizing of Ms. Sonia Montecino

Aguirre and her political sympathies. From the moment of the narrative's inception, the figure of "the other," Lucinda Nahuelhual, is only
that, a figure, an empty signifier, a narration constructed on the significance of Ms. Aguirre's own political agenda. . . . the idea of "elevating"
the Mapuche woman, Lucinda, to the status of a signifier of an urban
feminist movement where power is maintained primarily within the
hands of "enlightened" women from the hegemony requires that the
indigenous woman accept a position of loss in order to signify meaning
to her audience of "sisters."[24]

Because I have not read *Los sueños,* I cannot comment on the specif-
ics of Millet's critique. But although it is true that there are possibilities
of distortion and misrepresentation involved in testimonio, the argument
here seems to reject the possibility of any textual representation of an
"other" as such (all signifiers are "empty" unless and until they signify
something for somebody) in favor of something like a (liberal?) notion of
the irreducible particularity of the individual. In a situation such as that
of Chile today, politically the question would seem not so much one of
the differences in the social situations of the direct narrator and the interlocutor, but rather one of the possibility of their articulation together in a
common program or front that at the same time would advance women's
rights and the rights of the indigenous groups, without subordinating one
to the other.

In the creation of the testimonial text, control of representation does
not flow only one way, as Millet's argument implies: someone like Rigoberta Menchú is also in a sense exploiting her interlocutor in order to
have her story reach and influence an international audience, something
that, as an activist for her community, she sees in quite utilitarian terms
as a political task. Moreover, editorial power does not belong to the compiler alone. Menchú, worrying, correctly, that there are some ways in
which her account could be used against her or her people (for example,
by academic specialists advising counterinsurgency programs such as
the CIA set up in Guatemala), notes that there are certain things—her
Nahuatl name, for example—she will not speak of: "I'm still keeping my
Indian identity a secret. I'm still keeping secret what I think no one should
know. Not even anthropologists or intellectuals, no matter how many
books they have, can find out all our secrets."[25] Although Burgos-Debray
does the final selection and shaping of the text, the individual narrative
units are wholly composed by Menchú and, as such, depend on her skills
and intentionality as a narrator. An example of this may be found in the
excruciating detail she uses (in chapters 24 and 27) to describe the torture

and murder of her mother and brother by the Guatemalan army, detail that gives the episodes a hallucinatory and symbolic intensity different from the matter-of-fact narration one expects from testimonio. One could say this is a kind of testimonial expressionism, or "magic realism."

Perhaps something like Mao's notion of "contradictions among the people" (as opposed to contradictions between "the people" as a whole and imperialism, as in the case of the Chinese war against Japanese occupation) expresses the nature of the narrator/compiler/reader relations in the testimonio, in the sense that there are deep and inescapable contradictions involved in these relations, contradictions that can be resolved only on the level of general structural change on both national and global levels. But there is also a sense of sisterhood and mutuality in the struggle against a common system of oppression. Testimonio is not, in other words, a reenactment of the anthropological function of the colonial or subaltern "native informant," about which Spivak, among others, has written. Hence, although one of the sources and models of the testimonio is undoubtedly the ethnographic "life history," it is not reducible to that category (nor, as noted earlier, to oral history).[26]

One fact that is evident in the passage from *I, Rigoberta Menchú* under discussion is that the presence of a "real" popular voice in the testimonio is at least in part an illusion. Obviously, we are dealing here, as in any discursive medium, with an effect that has been produced, in the case of a testimonio by both the direct narrator—using devices of an oral story-telling tradition—and the compiler, who, according to norms of literary form and expression, makes a text out of the material. Although it is easy to deconstruct this illusion, it is also necessary to insist on its presence to understand the testimonio's peculiar aesthetic-ideological power. Elzbieta Sklodowska, developing a point about the textual nature of testimonio that can be connected with the argument made by Millet, cautions that:

> it would be naive to assume a direct homology between text and history. The discourse of a witness cannot be a reflection of his or her experience, but rather a refraction determined by the vicissitudes of memory, intention, ideology. The intention and the ideology of the author-editor further superimpose the original text, creating more ambiguities, silences, and absences in the process of selecting and editing the material in a way consonant with norms of literary form. Thus, although the testimonio uses a series of devices to gain a sense of veracity and authenticity—among them the point of view of the first-person witness-narrator—the play between fiction and history reappears inexorably as a problem.[27]

What is at stake, however, is the particular nature of the "reality effect" of the testimonio, not simply the difference between (any) text and reality. What is important about testimonio is that it produces, if not the real, then certainly a sensation of experiencing the real that has determinate effects on the reader that are different from those produced by even the most realist or "documentary" fiction. "More than an interpretation of reality," notes Jara in a useful corrective to Sklodowska's point, the testimonio is "a trace of the Real, of that history which, as such, is inexpressible."[28]

Sklodowska is right about the interplay between real and imaginary in testimonio. But to subsume testimonio under the category of literary fictionality is to deprive it of its power to engage the reader in the ways I have indicated here, to make of it simply another form of literature, as good as, but certainly no better than and not basically different from, what is already the case. This seems to me a formalist and, at least in effect, a politically liberal response to testimonio, which tolerates or encourages its incorporation into the academically sanctioned field of literature at the expense of relativizing its moral and political urgency.[29] What has to be understood, instead, is precisely how testimonio puts into question the existing institution of literature as an ideological apparatus of alienation and domination at the same time that it constitutes itself as a new form of literature.

Having said this much, however, I now need to distinguish testimonio from (1) that central form of nonfictional first-person narrative that is autobiography and cognate forms of personal narrative, such as memoirs, diaries, confessions, and reminiscences; and (2) Barbara Foley's articulation of the category of "documentary fiction" in *Telling the Truth*.[30] I will consider autobiography first, with the proviso that some of the forms of "documentary fiction" Foley considers are autobiographical or pseudoautobiographical. The dividing line between testimonio and autobiography is not always exact, but the following might represent the general case. Even in nineteenth-century memoirs of women or ex-slaves (that is, texts in which the narrator writes clearly from a position of subalternity), there is often implicit an ideology of individualism in the very convention of the autobiographical form, an ideology built on the notion of a coherent, self-evident, self-conscious, commanding subject who appropriates literature precisely as a means of "self-expression" and who in turn constructs textually for the reader the liberal imaginary of a unique, "free," autonomous ego as the natural form of being and public achievement. By contrast, as I have suggested, in testimonio the narrative "I" has the status of what linguists call a shifter—a linguistic function that can be assumed indiscriminately by anyone. Recalling Rigoberta

Menchú's narrative proposition, the meaning of her testimonio lies not in its uniqueness but in its ability to stand for the experience of her community as a whole. Because the authorial function has been erased or mitigated, the relationship between authorship and forms of individual and hierarchical power in bourgeois society has also changed. Testimonio represents an affirmation of the individual subject, even of individual growth and transformation, but in connection with a group or class situation marked by marginalization, oppression, and struggle. If it loses this connection, it ceases to be testimonio and becomes autobiography, that is, an account of, and also a means of access to, middle- or upper-class status, a sort of documentary bildungsroman. If Rigoberta Menchú had become a "writer" instead of remaining as she has a member of, and an activist for, her ethnic community, her narration would have been an autobiography. By contrast, even where the subject is a person "of the left," as, for example, in Agnes Smedley's *Daughter of the Earth,* Leon Trotsky's *My Life,* or Pablo Neruda's *Memoirs,* autobiography and the autobiographical novel are essentially conservative modes in the sense that they imply that individual triumph over circumstances is possible in spite of "obstacles." Autobiography produces in the reader—who, generally speaking, is already either middle- or upper-class or expecting to be—the specular effect of confirming and authorizing his or (less so) her situation of relative social privilege. Testimonio, by contrast, even in the case of testimonios from the political right, such as Armando Valladares's prison memoir *Against All Hope* or Solzhenitsyn's *Gulag Archipelago,* always signifies the need for a general social change in which the stability of the reader's world must be brought into question.[31]

As such, testimonio offers a kind of answer to the problem of women's access to literature. Sidonie Smith has argued that every woman who writes finally interrogates the ideology of gender that lies behind the engendering of self in forms such as the novel or autobiography.[32] She alludes to the notion that the institution of literature itself is phallocentric. On the other hand, repressing the desire for power in order to avoid complicity with domination is a form of female self-effacement sanctioned by the patriarchy. How do we find forms of expression that break out of this double bind? Many of the best-known testimonios are in the voices of women, yet, because of the narrative situation I have identified, testimonio does not produce textually an essentialized "woman's experience." It is a self-conscious instance of what Spivak has advocated as "strategic essentialism" in feminist political practice.[33]

I am generally sympathetic with the project Barbara Foley has staked out in *Telling the Truth.* In particular, her deconstruction of what she calls "the fact/fiction distinction" and her emphasis on the inevitable his-toricity of literary categories are useful for conceptualizing some aspects of the testimonio, including its peculiar truth claim on the reader. What Foley is not doing in *Telling the Truth,* however, is producing an account of testimonial narrative as such. Although some of the texts she discusses in her chapter on African American narrative are testimonios in the sense outlined here, Foley herself prefers to deal with them through the some-what different category of the documentary novel. But this is to make of testimonio one of the mutations the novel has undergone in the course of its (European) evolution from the Renaissance on, whereas I have wanted to suggest that it implies a radical break (as in the structuralist notion of *coupure*) with the novel and with literary fictionality as such. In other words, the testimonio is not a form of the novel. It cannot be adequately theorized, therefore, by the sort of argument Foley develops, which is, nonetheless, very useful for understanding certain forms of fiction and fictionalized autobiography that depend on the semiotic intensification of a reality effect.[34]

If the novel is a closed and private form in the sense that both the story and the subject end with the end of the text, defining that auto-referential self-sufficiency that is the basis of formalist reading practices, the testimonio exhibits by contrast what René Jara calls a "public inti-macy" *(intimidad pública)* in which the boundary between public and private spheres of life essential in all forms of bourgeois culture and law is transgressed.[35] The narrator in testimonio is a real person who continues living and acting in a real social history that also continues. Testimonio can never in this sense create the illusion of that textual in-itselfness that has been the basis of literary formalism, nor can it be adequately ana-lyzed in these terms. It is, to use Umberto Eco's slogan, an "open work" that implies the importance and power of literature as a form of social action, but also its radical insufficiency.

In principle, testimonio appears therefore as an extraliterary or even antiliterary form of discourse. That, paradoxically, is precisely the basis of both its aesthetic and its political appeal. As Foley suggests, in literary history the intensification of a narrative or representational reality effect is generally associated with the contestation of the dominant system and its forms of cultural idealization and legitimation. This was certainly the case of the picaresque novel and *Don Quixote* in relation to the novels of chivalry in the Spanish Renaissance. What happens, however, when something like testimonio is appropriated by (or as) "literature"? Does this involve a neutralization of testimonio's peculiar aesthetic effect, which depends, as we have seen, precisely on its status outside accepted literary forms and norms? In relation to these questions and the discussion of Foley above, I need finally to distinguish testimonio from the testimonial novel. Miguel Barnet calls his *Autobiography of a Runaway Slave* a "testimonial novel" *(novela testimonio),* even though the story is nonfictional.[36] In so doing, he emphasizes how the material of an ethnographic "life history" can be made into literature. But I would rather reserve the term "testimonial novel" (or Capote's "nonfiction novel") for those narrative texts in which an "author" in the conventional sense has either invented a testimonio-like story or, as in the case of *In Cold Blood* (or Barnet's own later work, *Canción de Rachel*), extensively reworked, with explicitly literary goals (greater figurative density, tighter narrative form, elimination of digressions and interruptions, and so on), a testimonial account that is no longer present except in its simulacrum. If the picaresque novel was the pseudoautobiography of a lower-class individual (thus inverting a "learned" humanist form into a pseudopopular one), we might observe in recent literature (1) novels that are in fact pseudo-testimonios, inverting a form that grows out of subaltern experience into one that is middlebrow (an example might be the Mexican novel *Las aventuras, desaventuras y sueños de Adonis García: El vampiro de la Colonia Roma,* by Luis Zapata, which purports to be the testimonio of a homosexual prostitute); (2) a growing concern on the part of contemporary novelists to produce something like a testimonial "voice" in their fiction, with variable political intentions (for example, Mario Vargas Llosa's *The Story of Mayta* on the right, Manlio Argueta's *One Day of Life* on the left); and (3) a series of ambiguous forms located between the novel and testimonio as such (for example, Nawal El Saadawi's *Woman at Point Zero* or the very intriguing novel/memoir of the Cultural Revolution, Yang Jiang's *A Cadre School Life,* which is a testimonio rendered in the mold of a narrative genre of classical Chinese literature).

But if the testimonio comes into being necessarily at the margin of the historically given institution of literature, it is also clear that it is becoming a new postfictional form of literature, with significant cultural and political repercussions. To return to our starting point: if the novel had a special relationship with humanism and the rise of the European bourgeoisie, testimonio is by contrast a new form of narrative literature in which we can at the same time witness and be a part of the emerging culture of an international proletarian/popular-democratic subject in its period of ascendancy. But it would be in the spirit of testimonio itself to end on a more skeptical note: literature, even where it is infused with a popular-democratic form and content, as in the case of testimonio, is not itself a popular-democratic cultural form, and (pace Gramsci) it is an open question as to whether it can ever be. How much of a favor do we do testimonio by positing, as here, that it has become a new form of literature or by making it an alternative reading to the canon (one track of the Stanford Western culture requirement now includes *I, Rigoberta Menchú*)? Perhaps such moves preempt or occlude a vision of an emergent popular-democratic culture that is no longer based on the institutions of humanism and literature.

(1989)

2
"Through All Things Modern": Second Thoughts on Testimonio

This is why Indians are thought to be stupid. They can't think, they don't know anything, they say. But we have hidden our identity because we needed to resist, we wanted to protect what governments have wanted to take away from us. They have tried to take our things away and impose others on us, be it through religion, through dividing up the land, through schools, through books, through radio, through all things modern.[1]

To situate the title and the quote: these are second thoughts both on the testimonio itself and on my own work on testimonio, represented by my essay "The Margin at the Center."[2] I wrote there that by testimonio I understand a novel- or novella-length narrative told in the first person by a narrator who is also the real-life protagonist or witness of the events he or she recounts. In recent years it has become an important, perhaps the dominant, form of literary narrative in Latin America. The best-known example available in English translation is the text that the passage above comes from, *I, Rigoberta Menchú,* the life story of a young Guatemalan indian woman, which, as she puts it in her presentation, is intended to represent "the reality of a whole people."[3]

I want to start with the fact of the February 1990 elections in Nicaragua, which reminds us of Fredric Jameson's redefinition of Lacan's category of the Real as that which hurts. A decade after the revolutionary high tide of 1979–81, it is clear that the moment of optimism about the possibilities for rapid social transformation in Central America has passed. Whether this represents a new, postrevolutionary stage in that region's history or simply a recession before the appearance of a new cycle of radicalization—perhaps also involving Mexico this time—is open to question. Testimonios like *I, Rigoberta Menchú*, or Omar Cabezas's *Fire from the Mountain* and Margaret Randall's *Sandino's Daughters* from Nicaragua were very much part of the literary imaginary of international solidarity with or critical support for the Central American revolutions. So the electoral defeat of the Sandinistas, while it is certainly not absolute— there is still quite a bit of room for maneuver and struggle—must force us in any case to reconsider the relation between testimonio, liberation struggles, solidarity work, and academic pedagogy. I want to center this reconsideration in particular on the question of the relation of testimonio to the field of literature. This will in turn connect with some questions about what it is we do in the humanities generally, and particularly in connection with Latin American and Third World literatures.

I ended my reflection on the testimonio in "The Margin at the Center" with the thought that

> literature, even where it is infused with a popular-democratic form
> and content, as in the case of testimonio, is not in itself a popular-
> democratic cultural form, and (pace Gramsci) it is an open question as
> to whether it ever can be. How much of a favor do we do testimonio
> by positing, as here, that it has become a new form of literature or by
> making it an alternative reading to the canon (one track of the Stanford
> Western culture requirement now includes *I, Rigoberta Menchú*)? Per-
> haps such moves preempt or occlude a vision of an emergent popular-
> democratic culture that is no longer based on the institutions of human-
> ism and literature. (26)

I might have added "no longer based, that is, on the university," because I believe that literature and the university (in the historically specific form each takes during and after the Renaissance) have been, appearances to the contrary, mutually dependent on each other, and as such deeply implicated in the processes of state formation and colonial expansion that define early-modern Europe. This legacy still marks each, making their interaction in contemporary processes of decolonization and postcoloniality at the same time both necessary and problematic.

Testimonios are in a sense made for people like us, in that they allow us to participate as academics and yuppies, without leaving our studies and classrooms, in the concreteness and relativity of actual social struggles ("we," "our," and "us" designate here the readers—or potential readers—of this essay). To borrow a passage from Bakhtin's definition of prose art in his essay "Discourse in the Novel" (with thanks to Barbara Harlow for bringing it to my attention), testimonios are texts whose discourses are "still warm from the struggle and hostility, as yet unresolved and still fraught with hostile intentions and accents." But they are (putting Derrida in parenthesis here) still also *just* texts and not actual warm or, in the case of the victims of the death squads, not so warm bodies. I am not trying to guilt-trip people about being academics and yuppies. I am both. Russell Jacoby's critique of the academic encapsulation of the left is wrong; the university is an absolutely crucial and central institution of late-capitalist society. I believe in Gramsci's slogan of a long march through the institutions, and it follows that I think that our battlefield is the classroom and conference hall, that the struggle over the teaching and interpretation of literature has something to do with the production of new forms of ideological hegemony. As a pedagogic issue, the use of testimonio has to do concretely with the possibility of interpellating our students (and all readers are or were at one time students) in a relation of solidarity with liberation movements and human rights struggles, both here in the United States and abroad.

In the theoretical discussion on testimonio, much deconstructive zeal has been spent on the fact that it is a mediated narrative: as in the case of *I, Rigoberta Menchú*, an oral narrative told by a speaker from a sub-altern or "popular" social class or group to an interlocutor who is an intellectual or professional writer from the middle or upper class (and in many cases from a different ethno-linguistic position: the equivalent of what Peruvians call a *pituco*—white, upper-class, culturally European, etc.), who then, according to this subject position, edits and textualizes the account, making it available to a similarly positioned national and international reading public as a printed book or pamphlet. The possi-bilities for distortion and/or co-optation in such a situation are many, as Gayatri Spivak has suggested in "Can the Subaltern Speak?" But one of the things that can be said in its favor is that it can serve as both an allegorical figure for, and a concrete means of, the union of a radicalized (Marxist) intelligentsia with the subaltern. Moreover, it is a relationship in which neither of the participants has to cancel its identity as such. Testimonios have become, in certain sorts of conjunctures, a discursive space where the possibilities of such an alliance can be negotiated on both sides without too much angst about otherness or "othering." Spivak is correct that "contemporary invocations of 'libidinal economy' and desire as the determining interest, combined with the practical politics of the oppressed (under socialized capital) 'speaking for themselves,' restore the category of the sovereign subject within the theory that seems most to question it."[4] But this is more a question—and not a simple one at that—of the ideology of the consumers of testimonio rather than its producers. Moreover, political struggle involves not only the critique of the forms of the dominant ideology but also the necessarily ideological production of new forms of identity. As Doris Sommer has noted, "But to read women's testimonials, curiously, is to mitigate the tension between First World 'self' and Third World 'other.' I do not mean this as a license to deny the differences, but as a suggestion that the testimonial subject may be a model for respectful, nontotalizing politics."[5]

I understand, of course, that "literature" is itself a matter of semiosis: of who defines what counts under what institutional circumstances. The political question is what is gained or lost by including or excluding under this name particular kinds of discursive practice. As in the Stanford Western culture requirements, the pedagogic incorporation of testimonio in the academy has involved strategically a theoretical-critical struggle to define it not just as an ethnographic document or "life history" but as part of the canon of Great Works through which the humanist subject as such is formed in a modern, multicultural curriculum.[6] The authorizing operation of literary criticism, including "The Margin at the Center," in this regard has been to articulate testimonio as a form of "minor" literature particularly sensitive to the representation or expression of subalternity. Fredric Jameson gives it his imprimatur as an alternative to what he terms the "overripe subjectivity" of the bildungsroman; Barbara Harlow makes it a key form of "resistance literature"; Cornell publishes Barbara Foley's book on "documentary fiction"—a category that subsumes the testimonio; Margaret Randall offers a "how-to" manual for would-be practitioners of the form; George Yúdice sees it as a Third World form of a postmodernism of resistance; Juan Duchesne writes a doctoral dissertation at SUNY-Albany on Latin American guerrilla narratives; Gayatri Spivak and Elzbieta Sklodowska caution against a naive reception of the form; and so on.[7] Even to arrive at the situation we are now in, where it has become fashionable to deconstruct in de Manian fashion this or that testimonio (Roberto González Echevarría was the pioneer of this in his article on Miguel Barnet's *Autobiography of a Runaway Slave*),[8] still is to give it, in effect, a status as a literary text comparable to, say, Rousseau's *Confessions*.

This is fine and basically correct as far as I am concerned. There is no reason to suppose that Rousseau has anything more to tell us than Rigoberta Menchú or Esteban Montejo, the narrator of the *Autobiography of a Runaway Slave*. But we must also understand why testimonio comes into being outside or at the margin of the historically constituted institution of literature in modern Western culture. At least part of its aesthetic effect—I mean this in precisely the Russian formalist sense of *ostranenie* or defamiliarization—is that it is *not* literary, not linguistically elaborated or authorial. One symptom of this has been an ambivalence about the "artistic" as opposed to the "documentary" character of testimonio, and about the distinction between testimonio per se and the more elaborated "testimonial novel" *(novela-testimonio),* such as those of Miguel Barnet (Capote's *In Cold Blood* would be an English-language equivalent).[9] Testimonio appears where the adequacy of existing literary forms and styles—even of the dominant language itself—for the representation of the subaltern has entered into crisis.[10] Even where its instrumentality is to reach in printed form a metropolitan reading public culturally and physically distant from the position and situation of its narrator, testimonio is not engendered out of the same humanist ideology of the literary that motivates its reception by this public or its incorporation into the humanities curriculum; and in some cases it actively resists being literature. Let me give two examples, one from a testimonio about the armed struggle in El Salvador, the other from *I, Rigoberta Menchú*.

Ana Guadalupe Martínez's testimonio *Las cárceles clandestinas de El Salvador* (The secret prisons of El Salvador) deals with her involvement in the Salvadoran guerrilla underground with the Ejército Revolucionario del Pueblo (ERP, Revolutionary Army of the People) and her capture, torture, and imprisonment by the army. She insists that her account is "the result of a collective and militant effort, and *has no intellectual or literary pretensions*; it is a contribution to the ideological development and formation of cadres on the basis of concrete experience that should be discussed and analyzed by those who are consistently immersed in the making of the revolution." Her co-prologuist, René Cruz, similarly notes: "There is considerable concrete experience which has been lost by not being processed and transmitted by militants, and another large part has been deformed in its essence by being elaborated by leftist intellectual intermediaries who adjust what they are relating not in relation to revolutionary needs but *in relation to the needs of fiction and bourgeois revolutionary theorizing.*"[11]

The point about "no intellectual pretensions" is disingenuous, and there is more than a trace here of the intense sectarianism that has marked

the Salvadoran revolutionary movement. "Leftist intellectual intermediaries" alludes to the most famous modern Salvadoran writer, Roque
Dalton, who also worked in testimonial forms, and who, as it happens,
was Martínez's adversary in an internal debate in the ERP in the mid-
1970s over the direction of the armed struggle (a debate that led to his
assassination by the leadership faction of the ERP that Martínez supported).[12] Still, her point is worth taking. She wants to do something
other than literature with her narrative and feels it would in some sense
be compromised or betrayed by becoming literature, whereas Dalton,
like Miguel Barnet, was concerned with the ideological and aesthetic
problems of making testimonio a form of left-modernist literature.

I, Rigoberta Menchú begins with a strategic disavowal of both literature and the liberal concept of the authority of private experience: "My
name is Rigoberta Menchú. I am twenty-three years old. This is my testimony. I didn't learn it from a book, and I didn't learn it alone" (1). The
quote at the start of this essay belongs with a series of passages in her text
where Menchú explicitly counterposes book learning to direct experience or attacks the presence of no doubt well-intentioned schoolteachers
in her village, arguing that they represent an agency of penetration and
destruction of the highland indian communities by the landowners and
the Guatemalan state. Here are some others:

> When children reach ten years old [in our village], that's the moment
> when their parents and the village leaders talk to them again. . . . It's
> also when they remind them that our ancestors were dishonored by the
> White Man, by colonization. But they don't tell them the way it's writ-
> ten down in books, because the majority of Indians can't read or write,
> and don't even know that they have their own texts. No, they learn
> it through oral recommendations, the way it has been handed down
> through the generations. (13)

> I had a lot of ideas but I knew I couldn't express them all. I wanted to
> read or write Spanish. I told my father this, that I wanted to learn to
> read. Perhaps things were different if you could learn to read. My father
> said, "Who will teach you? You have to find out by yourself, because
> I can't help you. I know of no schools and I have no money for them any-
> way." I told him that if he talked to the priests, perhaps they'd give me
> a scholarship. But my father said he didn't agree with that idea because I
> was trying to leave the community, to go far away, and find out what was
> best for me. He said: "You'll forget about our common heritage." . . . My
> father was very suspicious of schools and all that sort of thing. He gave

as an example the fact that many of my cousins had learned to read
and write but they hadn't been of use to the community. They try to
move away and feel different when they can read and write. (89)

Sometimes I'd hear how those teachers taught and what education
was like in the villages. They said that the arrival of the Spaniards was
a conquest, a victory, while we knew in practice that it was just the
opposite. . . . This taught me that even though a person may learn to
read and write, he should not accept the false education they give our
people. Our people must not think as the authorities think. (169–70)

When teachers come into the villages, they bring with them the ideas
of capitalism and getting on in life. They try and impose these ideas on
us. I remember that in my village there were two teachers for a while
and they began teaching the people, but the children told their parents everything they were being taught at school and the parents said:
"We don't want our children to become like *ladinos* [in Guatemala,
a Spanish-speaking white or mestizo]." And they made the teachers
leave. . . . For the Indian, it is better not to study than to become like
ladinos. (205)

One aspect of the archaeology of Menchú's position here involves the
Spanish practice during the Conquest of segregating the children of the
indian aristocracy from their families in order to teach them literacy and
Christian doctrine. Walter Mignolo has observed that this practice

shows that literacy is not instilled without violence. The violence, however, is not located in the fact that the youngsters have been assembled
and enclosed day and night. It comes, rather, from the interdiction of
having conversations with their parents, particularly with their mothers. In a primar[il]y oral society, in which virtually all knowledge is
transmitted by means of conversation, the preservation of oral contact
was contradictory with the effort to teach how to read and write. Forbidding conversations with the mother meant, basically, depriving the
children of the living culture imbedded in the language and preserved
and transmitted in speech.[13]

But it is not that, coming from a predominantly oral culture, Rigoberta
Menchú does not value literacy or formal education at all. Part of the
oedipal struggle with her father recounted in her story involves precisely
her desire, and eventually success, as a teenager at learning first to memo-
rize, then read, passages from the Bible in order to become a Catholic lay

catechist (just as later she would learn Spanish and several other indian languages because of the exigencies of her work as a peasant organizer, and would lead a fight to have a school built in her community).[14] It is rather, as these passages suggest, that she does not accept literacy and book learning, or the narrative of cultural and linguistic moderniza- tion they entail, as either adequate or *normative* cultural modes. She is conscious, among other things, of the holistic relation between the individualization produced by the government schools and the attempts to impose on her community an agrarian reform based on private owner- ship of parcels (as opposed to its tradition of communal ownership and sharing of resources). That is why she remains a testimonial narrator rather than an "author"—a subject position that in fact would imply, as in the case of Richard Rodriguez's memoir *Hunger of Memory,* a self- imposed separation from her community and culture of birth (and a loss or change of name). As Doris Sommer has shown, even in the act of ad- dressing us through the literary artifice of the testimonio—which is built on the convention of truth telling and openness—Menchú is also con- sciously withholding information from us, on the grounds that it could be used against her and her people by academically trained or advised counterinsurgency specialists.[15] Menchú is aware, in other words, of something we may have forgotten since the Vietnam War: the complicity of the university in cultural (and sometimes actual) genocide. The con- cluding words of her testimonio are "I'm still keeping secret what I think no one should know. Not even anthropologists or intellectuals, no matter how many books they have, can find out all our secrets" (247).

We could say that Menchú *uses* the testimonio as literature without subscribing to a humanist ideology of the literary, or, what amounts to the same thing, without abandoning her identity and role as an indian activist to become a professional writer. This may be one way of answer- ing Spivak's question in "Can the Subaltern Speak?" No, not as such (because "the subaltern is the name of the place which is so displaced . . . that to have it speak is like Godot arriving on a bus").[16] But the testimo- nial narrator, like Rigoberta Menchú, is not the subaltern as such either, rather something more like an "organic intellectual" of the subaltern who speaks to the hegemony by means of a metonymy of self in the name and in the place of it. Testimonio is located at the intersection of the cultural forms of bourgeois humanism, like literature and the printed book, en- gendered by the academy and colonialism and imperialism, and subaltern cultural forms. It is not an authentic expression of the subaltern (whatever that might be),[17] but it is not (or should not be) easily assimilable to, or collectible *as,* literature either.

My work with Marc Zimmerman on the role of poetry in Central American revolutionary movements showed that it was not just a reflection or expression of an already constituted ideology, but rather a precondition for its elaboration; that something like the Sandinista revolution in Nicaragua depended in some significant ways on developments in modern Nicaraguan poetry initiated by the Granada Vanguardists in the 1930s under the influence of U.S. modernists such as Stevens, Pound, and Eliot; that, in a strikingly postmodern way, literature was not only a means of revolutionary politics but also a model for it in Central America.[18] Why this was the case had to do not only with the content of individual texts (i.e., with something that might be revealed by a hermeneutic or deconstructive analysis), but also with the way literature itself was positioned as a social practice by processes of combined and uneven development in Central American history.

As the late Ángel Rama argued, a "republic of letters" *(ciudad letrada)* and the consequent normative role of literature and of the writer are among the basic forms of institutional continuity between colonial and contemporary Latin America.[19] The availability of literary texts through the medium of the printed book to an "ideal reader" is a historically and ethnically specific one, linked in Europe to the rise of the middle class, the commodification of literary production and distribution, and the corresponding growth of democratic forms of public education and a reading public, particularly in the nineteenth century. The mode of existence of literature in a caste-ridden, quasi-feudal society like colonial Latin America was, in several respects, quite different than this. To begin with, as Mignolo's comment illustrates, literature was itself a colonial import, with little or no continuity whatever with pre-Columbian discursive practices (where they existed, pre-Columbian texts were systematically destroyed). Most people in the colonies—perhaps 80 to 90 percent of the population—did not read at all, and many had no or only a rudimentary grasp of even spoken Spanish or Portuguese. In contrast to our contemporary concern with illiteracy (with its implicit equation of literacy, modernization, and democratization), however, this was regarded as a normal, even desirable, state of affairs. Access to written texts in Spanish or Latin was in itself a mark of distinction that separated colonizer from colonized, rulers from ruled, European from native.[20]

This was not just a question of functional literacy, however. The colonial fashion for the highly wrought and complex poetry represented by fashionable metropolitan models like Góngora involved the fetishization of writing as an aristocratic or sublime activity because it eluded, by its difficulty, the comprehension not only of the illiterate, but also of those

who might be functionally literate but were not university-educated—
sectors of the indigenous population to begin with, but also lower-class
Creoles and the *castas* or mixed-bloods. What such a literature transmitted to its readers—the *letrados* or men of letters (for they were
almost always men)—in the urban centers of the colonial viceroyalties
was not only a sign of aristocratic worth *(honor)* and connection to a
distant metropolitan center, but also a technique of power, an exercise
or formal simulacrum of the ability to discern, organize, sublimate, and
ultimately control productively. This situation affected in part the nature
of the literary text itself as a cultural artifact. In general, secular writing
in the colonies was not intended for commercial publication and even
less for a general reading public. There were printing establishments in
the colonies, but—even at the end of the seventeenth century—a major
project like the first anthology of the poetry of Sor Juana Inés de la Cruz
required publication in Spain. It was common for literary texts to be
available only in hand-lettered manuscript copies circulated privately to
individual readers or special audiences *(tertulias)*.

In its very form of circulation, then, but also in the cultivation of
extreme forms of pedantry and linguistic complexity, Latin American
colonial literature was not something intended for or available to everyone, certainly not for a socially amorphous public that could lay hold of
it through the market in books. Literature (less anachronistically, *letras*,
including, for example, history, biography, sermons, letters, and, especially, the essay), in other words, not only had a central role in the self-
representation of the upper and upper-middle strata of Latin American
colonial society; it was one of the social practices by which such strata
constituted themselves as dominant. That is why for a neo-Machiavellian
political theorist and moralist like the Jesuit Baltasar Gracián an "art of
wit" *(arte de agudeza)* based on the study of literary conceits *(concep-
tos)* was a prerequisite for the formation of the Baroque man of affairs.
(In general, it was via the curricula established by Jesuit pedagogy at the
end of the sixteenth and the beginning of the seventeenth century that
innovations in literature found their way into the hearts and minds of the
colonial intelligentsia.)

This very acute sense of the power of literature—which involves both
a recognition and an overvaluation of its cultural importance—accounts
for the prohibition by the colonial authorities of both the publication and
the importation of novels: the novel was quite literally seen as a medium
incompatible with the assumptions of colonial rule (although it could,
with heavy censorship, be tolerated in Spain and Portugal). This anomaly,
however, also made of literature a place where the ambitions and resent-

ments of Creoles, mestizos, and in some cases indians and slaves or for-mer slaves could begin to take shape. The colonial intellectual was in the position of having to mediate in his or her writing between an empirically vivid American reality and an increasingly absent and abstract European model of civilization represented by literature. As in the case of the pro-hibition of the novel, problems of genre, style, decorum, neologism, and so on could easily become entangled and confused with political and social problems, and literature itself became both a sign of the colony's connection to metropolitan centers in Spain and Portugal (themselves, it should be remembered, only dubiously and recently European) and a practical medium for the elaboration of an ultimately anticolonial sensi-bility among the Creole upper and middle classes.

The later eighteenth century brought into this scene the sometimes clandestine influence of Neoclassicism and Enlightenment literary models, Free Masonry, the Black Legend, Manchester School political economy, the French Revolution, and so on. But in a gesture of formal continuity with the colony, literature was also to be marked as a form of republi-can institutionality during the independence struggles of the nineteenth century. Latin American liberals—themselves formed pedagogically as *letrados*—saw the development of literature as a way to create a mentali-ty appropriate for the consolidation under their authority of the newly independent republics. The new "national" literatures of Latin America therefore emerged in close connection both to state formation and to the *letrados*' own formation and incorporation into the state as, simultaneous-ly, an intelligentsia and an actual or would-be ruling class. The literatures evolved with the process of social differentiation and status struggle of the members of this intelligentsia. The literatures served to define the *letrados*' group and personal identity, relationship to power and to other social classes or groups, sense of the defects and possibilities of development of the new societies, and, in a sort of feedback effect, belief in the central role of literature and literary culture in assuring that development. But by re-imposing, now under quasi-democratic and modernizing auspices, writing and literacy as standards of cultural performance, this liberal-Romantic cult of literature put the predominantly oral practices of song and nar-rative of the indigenous population (a majority in some countries) and the mestizo peasantry and rural proletariat in a relation of subordination and domination, deepening the separation between a hegemonic Spanish-language print-based culture and subaltern cultures and languages that had been introduced with the colonial institution of literature.[21]

The continued centrality of literature as a cultural form in Latin Ameri-can society, revealed in the popularity of and critical hoopla about Boom narrative, involves something like a modernist (in the English-language sense of the term) revision of this ideology of the literary in its colonial and republican variants. In this revision, the development of new forms of literature is seen as intimately bound up with economic and social modernization, by providing an agency for a progressive process of transculturation—the term was coined by the Cuban ethnographer Fernando Ortíz to describe the interaction of European and African elements in the formation of Cuban culture—involving a sometimes agonic, sometimes beneficent synthesis of European and non-European, high and low, urban and rural, intellectual and popular cultural forms. Ángel Rama was the most explicit proponent of this concept on the left, relating it to the tasks of national liberation struggle in the 1960s, but in one way or another it has tended to characterize Latin American literary criticism generally during the Boom and after (there is a neoconservative version of it in Octavio Paz, Emir Rodríguez Monegal, or Mario Vargas Llosa, for example). Directly or indirectly connected to this concept is the almost unchallenged assumption in Latin American literary history—its origins are in the work of Pedro Henríquez Ureña, the founder of modern Latin American literary criticism—that the writing of the colonial and independence periods represents a proto-nationalistic process of cultural *mestizaje* and differentiation. As Julio Ramos has noted, this assumption, which made literature and literary values the key signifiers of Latin American nationality for a national-bourgeois intelligentsia, became institutionalized as part of the ideology of the humanities in the Spanish-American university system in the early twentieth century, precisely as a response to the perceived threat represented by proletarianization and U.S.-style mass culture.[22]

I don't want to place myself in the position of denying the sometimes progressive role of literature and the humanities in Latin American society: among other things, such a position would undermine the argument I tried to develop in my book on Central American revolutionary literature mentioned earlier. At the same time, the aversion or ambivalence of the testimonio toward literature that we have noted here (and, in a related way, the failure of the poetry workshop experiment in the Nicaraguan revolution championed by Ernesto Cardenal) suggests not only that cultural democratization must involve a transformation of literature's dominant forms and character—most particularly a breakdown and renegotiation of the distinctions on which its status as a master discourse have rested—but also that literature itself (along with the concomitant standards and practice of "good writing") may in the process lose its centrality and authority as a cultural practice.

There is a critical moment in the introduction to *I, Rigoberta Menchú* where the interlocutor, the Venezuelan social scientist Elisabeth Burgos, debates with herself about what to correct in the transcription of the recordings of Menchú's conversations with her. She decides to leave in, for example, repetitions and digressions that she considers characteristic of oral narrative but, on the other hand, "to correct the gender mistakes which inevitably occur when someone has just learned to speak a foreign language. It would have been artificial to leave them uncorrected and it would have made Rigoberta look 'picturesque,' which is the last thing I wanted" (xx–xxi).

One might object here that the interlocutor is manipulating the material the informant provides to suit her own metropolitan political, intellectual, and aesthetic predilections, were it not for the fact this is not something Menchú herself would have resisted or resented, since her point in telling her story to Burgos was precisely to make it available to reading publics both in Guatemala and abroad. For what has happened between Menchú's speech act and Burgos's preface is that her narrative has become both a "text" and "literary." There is perhaps no more mediated and editorially mutilated testimonial text in Latin American literature than the *Autobiography* of the Cuban ex-slave Juan Francisco Manzano, which was prepared in 1835 at the urging of the Cuban liberal Domingo Del Monte, corrected and edited by the overtly abolitionist novelist Anselmo Suaréz y Romero, and subsequently abridged and translated into English for a metropolitan audience by the major agent of British imperialism in Cuba, Richard Madden. Sylvia Molloy has compared the unedited version of Manzano's original, handwritten manuscript with the published versions in Spanish and English. She concludes:

> The *Autobiografía* as Manzano wrote it, with its run-in sentences, breathless paragraphs, dislocated syntax and idiosyncratic misspellings, vividly portrays that quandary—an anxiety of origins, ever renewed, that provides the text with the stubborn, uncontrolled energy that is possibly its major achievement. The writing, *in itself,* is the best self-portrait we have of Manzano, his greatest contribution to literature; at the same time, it is what translators, editors and critics cannot tolerate. . . . [The] notion (shared by many) that there is a clear narrative imprisoned, as it were, in Manzano's *Autobiografía,* waiting for the hand of the cultivated editor to free it from the slag—this notion that the impure text must be replaced by a clean (white?) version of it to be readable—amounts to another, aggressive mutilation, that of denying the text readability in its own terms.[23]

Can we take this, mutatis mutandis, as an allegory of both the production of testimonio and its incorporation into the humanities? What
was at stake in the Stanford debate about the core curriculum was the
opposition of two different canons or reading lists—one traditional and
Euro- and phallocentric, the other Third Worldist and feminist. But literature and the humanities as such—not to speak of Stanford's function
in the formation and reproduction of class power in the U.S. and global
economy—were never put into question. They were, rather, the condition
of possibility of struggle over the curriculum and the reading lists in the
first place. I understand this position, and it is one I pursue in my own
work of presenting and interpreting texts in the classroom (which has
included teaching courses on Central American revolutionary literature
at, among other places, Stanford).

But in dealing with the testimonio I have also begun to discover in
myself a kind of posthumanist agnosticism about literature. I am not
proposing that there is any more authentic or culturally effective ground
than the one we are on as producers and students of literature in the
academy, and in any case ideologies (even literary ones), like neuroses,
defend themselves with very powerful and effective systems of resistance:
nothing you experience in an essay of this sort is going to make you reconsider what you fundamentally believe. But in spite of Ernesto Laclau's
point, which I consider extremely important in other contexts, that ideological signifiers do not have a necessary "class-belonging," the problem
of testimonio indicates that literature cannot be simply appropriated by
this or that social project. It is deeply marked by its own historical and
institutional entanglements, its "tradition of service," so to speak. There
may come a time when we have a new community of things we can call
literature; but not now. Among the many lessons testimonio has to offer
us is one that suggests that it is no longer a question of "reading against
the grain," as in the various academic practices of textual deconstruction
we are familiar with, but of beginning to read against literature itself.

Addendum on Postmodernism and Testimonio

In a note (note 10) to "The Margin at the Center," I suggested a com-
plementarity between Latin American testimonio and First World postmodernism, writing that "The reception of testimonio thus has something
to do with a revulsion for fiction and the fictive as such, with its 'postmodern' estrangement."

Some second thoughts are perhaps also in order on this score. Clearly,
there is a problem in applying a term that is generally conceived in relation to the narcissism and anomie of post-Fordist capitalist societies to

those represented in much of Latin American and Third World testimonio, which either have not gone through the stage of "modernity" (in the Weberian sense) yet, or display an "uneven" modernity (what society does not, however?). Clearly, there is also a correspondence (sometimes quite direct, as in the case of architecture) between cultural phenomena identified as postmodernist and the present sensibility and strategies of multinational capitalism, which gives some credence to the idea that postmodernism may be a form of cultural imperialism. There is the related danger that the production of a "postmodernist sublime" in relation to Latin America may involve the aesthetic festishization, as in Joan Didion's *Salvador,* of its social, cultural, and economic status quo (as "abject," chaotic, carnivalesque, etc.), thereby attenuating the urgency for radical social change and displacing it onto cultural dilettantism and quietism. As George Yúdice has noted, the flux of late-capitalist commodity culture that is seen as liberating by postmodernist theorists like Jean Baudrillard may represent in fact new forms of oppression and subalternity for Third World peoples as it restructures and re-semiotizes their cultures. In the same vein, there is Neil Larsen's useful warning that, even where there is a "promise of subversion" in postmodernism, this "seems no more and no less genuine than that long-ago discredited pledge of the modernist vanguard to, as it were, seize hold of capital's cultural and psychic mechanisms without firing a shot."[24]

However, I think there is also an important sense in which the forms of popular-democratic cultural resistance to imperialism represented by and in testimonio themselves rise up on a postmodern terrain.[25] The two interrelated problematics that are generally taken as defining postmodernism are the collapse of the distinction between elite and popular (or mass) cultures, sometimes expressed as the loss of aesthetic autonomy (Jameson); and the collapse of the "great narratives" of "Western" progress and enlightenment—including both bourgeois and Marxist historicisms—with which the specifically aesthetic project of modernism was associated. Similarly, the aesthetic and ideological significance of testimonio depends on its ability to function in the historically constituted space that separates elite and popular cultures in Latin America, and to generate postcolonial, non-Eurocentric narratives of individual and collective historical destiny. Where literature in Latin America has been (mainly) a vehicle for engendering an adult, white, male, patriarchal, "lettered" subject, testimonio allows the emergence—albeit mediated—of subaltern female, gay, indigenous, and proletarian "oral" identities. In this sense, it is coincident with postmodernism, rather than its other. It is true that part of what is designated as postmodernism is related to the rampant commodification and monopolization of even elite cultural production in late-capitalist societies, which also affects peripheral social formations (the small, national publishing houses that might have published Jorge Luis Borges as a young writer, for example, are being taken over or displaced by multinationals concerned with retailing translations of international best-sellers); at the same time, as Walter Benjamin understood, the loss of aura or desublimation of the artwork portended by mechanical reproduction can also be a very radical form of cultural democratization. Like testimonio, metropolitan postmodernism has involved in cultural production and consumption broad lower-middle-class, working-class, and minority sectors of the population previously excluded in general from and by high culture forms like literature.

The critique of postmodernism by Latin American leftists tends to set up a dichotomy between complex, antirepresentational, value-leveling, high-culture forms of literature of the sort represented by Borges or Boom narrative in general and simple, lineal, representational, value-affirming, "popular" narrative forms like the testimonio.[26] That some of the force of that dichotomy has necessarily crept into my own thinking about testimonio I think is evident from the preceding, but it needs also to be qualified. Although testimonio implies a challenge and an alternative to modernist literary models based on a subversion or rejection of narratives of identity, it is not, as we have seen, a completely autonomous form deriving directly from subaltern culture. It is (usually) a written transcription and textualization of a spoken narrative. The nature of any piece of writing—for example, the perceived qualities of testimonial as opposed to Boom narrative—is determined intertextually by its place in an already constituted discourse system. (Among the models Rigoberta Menchú mobilizes in constructing her testimonio is certainly biblical narrative, which as a Catholic lay catechist she knew intimately; there are clear traces of Omar Cabezas's readings of Boom novels as a university student in his *Fire from the Mountain,* a text "spoken" into a tape recorder; and so on.) Rather than a clear dichotomy between a purely oral popular culture of resistance and a purely colonial and/or neocolonial written high culture, Latin American culture has involved since the colonial period a series of shifts and transformations between elite and subaltern forms. In its very situation of enunciation, which separates radically the subject positions of the emitter and the receiver, testimonio is a form of the dialectic of oppressor and oppressed, involved in and constructed out of its opposing terms: master/slave, literature/oral narrative and song, metropolitan/national, European/indigenous or African, elite/popular, urban/rural, intellectual/manual work.

Testimonio is no more capable of transcending these oppositions than more purely "literary" forms of writing or narrative: that would require social and cultural transformations capable of initiating literacy campaigns and developing the educational and economic infrastructures necessary to create and sustain a mass reading public that have as a prior condition the victory of revolutionary movements in the first place. But testimonio does represent a new way of articulating these oppositions, and thus of defining new paradigms for the relationship between the intelligentsia and popular classes. In this sense, it represents also a new sort of aesthetic agency in political struggles.[27]

If, however, testimonio has been, in Latin America and elsewhere, the "literary" (under erasure) form of both revolutionary activism and more limited defensive struggles for human rights and re-democratization, paradoxically and against the expectations of its original protagonists, it does not seem particularly well suited to become the primary narrative form of an elaborated socialist society like Cuba, or even of periods of postrevolutionary consolidation and struggle, as in Nicaragua after 1979, perhaps because its very dynamics depend on the conditions of dramatic social and cultural inequality that fuel the revolutionary impulse in the first place. One of the problems revealed by the electoral defeat of the Sandinistas is that the identification portended in testimonio between a radicalized intelligentsia—represented by the FSLN leadership and upper and middle cadre—and the popular sectors had to some extent broken down. Coincidentally, one had begun to note a problematization of the formula of testimonio itself in Nicaragua: testimonios continued to be produced, but, except for those dealing with the contra war, they lacked the urgency of the testimonios of the revolutionary period (and testimonio must above all be a story that *needs* to be told, that involves some pressing and immediate problem of communication). We can conclude from this that, like postmodernism itself (and more particularly like its ancestor, the picaresque novel), testimonio is a transitional cultural form appropriate to processes of rapid social and historical change, but also destined to give way to different forms of representation as these processes move forward (or, as in the case of Nicaragua today, backward) to other stages, and the human collectivities that are their agents come into the possession of new forms of power and knowledge.

(1991)

3
The Real Thing

However unfeasible and inefficient it may
sound, I see no way to avoid insisting that
there has to be a simultaneous other focus;
not merely who am I? but who is the other
woman? How am I naming her? How does
she name me?

—*Gayatri Spivak*

This is an essay on Rigoberta Menchú and what she means, or does, for us. The title involves a perhaps overelaborate conceit, which may be forgiven someone who has spent a large part of his academic career studying the poetry of Góngora. It refers, on the one hand, to the phrase "the real thing" in American English (as in the advertising slogan "Coke is the real thing," which, of course, means something quite different if the reference is to the drug rather than the soft drink), and, on the other, to Lacan's concept of the Real as the order of "that which resists symbolization absolutely."

What may be less familiar is the sense Lacan, in his seminar *The Ethics of Psychoanalysis*, gave the capitalized form of the word *Thing*, following on the German *das Ding*. For Lacan, *das Ding*, which is to be distinguished from *Sache*—thing as "a product of industry and of human action as governed by language" in the sense of a created or linguistically elaborated object *(Wort)*—designates a traumatic otherness that cannot be represented or incorporated by the subject in language: the negative, in a sense, of the reassuring image the mirror or specular other—the face or presence of the parent or careperson—gives back to confirm "orthopedically," in Lacan's own image, the subject's either yet unformed or perpetually fading sense of itself in the mirror stage. The Thing is where the reality principle itself, in its connection to the pleasure principle and the regulatory function of the superego, founders.[1]

In an essay on *The Crying Game,* Slavoj Žižek elaborates the concept apropos Lacan's concern with the representation of the Lady in the discourse of courtly love as a tyrant "submitting her subjects to senseless, outrageous, impossible, arbitrary, capricious ordeals." This connects with Lacan's observation in the Seminar that the experience of the Mother as frustration by the subject described in Melanie Klein's account of early childhood is an instance of *das Ding.* In such representations, Žižek writes, "The Lady is thus as far as possible from any kind of purified spirituality." Rather,

> she functions as an inhuman partner in the precise sense of a radical Otherness which is wholly incommensurable with our needs and desires; as such she is simultaneously a kind of automaton, a machine which randomly utters meaningless demands. This coincidence of radical, inscrutable Otherness and pure machine is what confers on the Lady her uncanny, monstrous character—the Lady is the Other which is not our "fellow-creature," i.e. with whom no relation of empathy is possible. . . . The idealization of the Lady, her elevation to a spiritual, ethereal Ideal, is therefore to be conceived as a strictly secondary phenomenon, a narcissistic projection whose function is to render invisible her traumatic, intolerable dimension. . . . Deprived of every real substance, the Lady functions as a mirror onto which the subject projects his narcissistic ideal.[2]

The Lady in Question, then? Our Rigoberta? Why does it seem so natural, in our discourse about Rigoberta Menchú, to speak of her as Rigoberta? The use of the first name is appropriate, on the one hand, to address a friend or close family member, or, on the other, to address the subaltern. Is it that we are addressing Rigoberta Menchú as a friend in the work we do on her testimonio? We would not say with such ease, for example, Fred, for Fredric Jameson, unless we wanted to signify a personal relationship with him. Jameson himself (who continues to speak of Rigoberta, however) has noted that while testimonio involves the displacement of the "master subject" of modernist narrative, it does so paradoxically via the insistence on the first-person voice and proper name of the testimonial narrator.[3] The question of name—of the authority of a name—is, of course, embedded in the Spanish title of Menchú's testimonio, which reproduces its opening sentence, *Me llamo Rigoberta Menchú, y así me nació la conciencia*—My name is Rigoberta Menchú, and this is how my consciousness was formed—a title dramatically mistranslated in English as *I, Rigoberta Menchú: An Indian Woman in Guatemala*.

In her interview with Alice Brittin and Kenya Dworkin, which I will come back to several times here, Menchú insists on her right to appear as author or coauthor of *I, Rigoberta Menchú*: "[L]o que sí efectiva- mente es un vacío en el libro es el derecho de autor. . . . Porque la autoría del libro, efectivamente, debío ser más precisa, compartida, ¿verdad?" (What is in fact an absence in the book is the author's rights. . . . Because the authorship of the book, in fact, should have been more correctly indicated, shared, no?). Menchú is referring to the fact that Elisabeth Burgos, the Venezuelan anthropologist who acted as her interlocutor in the conversations in Paris that produced the text, appears in most edi- tions of the book as its author.[4]

In deference, then, to political correctness, not to say politeness or respect for a person I have met only formally, I always try to say or write Rigoberta Menchú or Menchú; but I have to keep reminding my- self on this score. My inclination, like yours, is to say Rigoberta—our Rigoberta—and I have to constantly censor this impulse. But of course, in another sense I would like to address Rigoberta Menchú as a *compa- ñera*, as we used to say Fidel or Che: that is, as someone who is in the same party or movement, someone who shares the struggle.

What is at stake in the question of how to address Rigoberta Menchú is the status of the testimonial narrator as a subject in her own right, rath- er than as someone who exists *for us*. What I have to say here is located in the tension between the injunction to grant Menchú the respect and autonomy she deserves as a human being in these terms, and the desire to see myself (my own projects and desires) in or through her. Do testi- monial narrators such as Rigoberta Menchú have a psyche, and would a psychoanalytic reading of their narratives be useful, or is the unconscious itself a form of what used to be called white-skin privilege? The ques- tion seems on the face of it impertinent, given the testimonial narrator's own insistence on the public and collective dimension of its narrative persona. Nevertheless, I would like to suggest that *I, Rigoberta Menchú* can (should) be read, without doing violence to the story, as an oedipal bildungsroman built around the working through of an Electra complex. The sequence of the narrative, which corresponds both to Menchú's com- ing of age and to the emergence of revolutionary armed struggle among the Mayan communities of Guatemala, goes from an initial rejection of the Mother and motherhood in favor of an Athena-like identification with the Father, Vicente, the campesino organizer;[5] but then also an authority struggle with the Father, who does not want his daughter to leave home and become educated; then the death of the Father at the hands of the repressive apparatus of the state, which leads to a possibility of identification with the Mother, now seen as an organizer; then the death of the Mother, again at the hands of the state; finally, in the act of narrating the testimonio itself, to the emergence of Menchú as a full speaking subject, an organizer and leader in her own right.

As in the case of Richard Rodriguez's *Hunger of Memory*, but with very different outcomes in terms of a sense of community, identity, and politics, *I, Rigoberta Menchú* not only narrates but embodies in its textual aporias the tensions involved in this almost classic "coming-of-age" sequence that marks the transition (or, perhaps more correctly, the oscillation) between the orders of the Imaginary and the Symbolic in the Lacanian schema of subject formation, local gemeinschaft and national or transnational gesellschaft, oral and print culture (Menchú telling her story orally and its textualization by Elisabeth Burgos), ethnographic narrative and "literature." Where, for Rodriguez, Spanish is the "maternal" language of the private sphere that has to be rejected in order to gain full access to the authority of the Symbolic order represented by English, so that *Hunger of Memory* is, among other things, a celebration of English writing programs and a critique of bilingualism, by contrast it is Menchú's contradictory and shifting relationship to her Mother, who represents the authority of oral culture and Mayan languages, as much as any specifically "political" experience, that is at the core of her own process of *concientización* as well as her ability to authorize herself as a narrator.[6]

At the (apparent) cost of relativizing the political-ethical claims *I, Rigoberta Menchú* makes on its readers, what my improvised psychoanalytic reading does is foreground its "complexity" as a text, the fact that its analysis is interminable, that it resists simply being the mirror that reflects back our narcissistic assumptions about what it should be. Despite all the misunderstandings her essay has provoked, this was surely Gayatri Spivak's point in answering the question "Can the Subaltern Speak?" paradoxically in the negative. By doing this, she was trying to show behind the good faith of the "committed" ethnographer or solidarity activist who "allows" or enables the subaltern to speak the trace of the colonial construction of an Other who is available to speak to us—with whom we *can* speak (that is, feel comfortable speaking with)—neutralizing thus the force of the reality of difference and antagonism.

Alberto Moreiras has suggested, following on Edward Said's *Orientalism,* the idea of "Latinamericanism" as an institutionally located discursive formation involved with constructing forms of representation and power—colonial or otherwise—*over* others. As in the case of Orientalism, Moreiras argues, Latinamericanism requires a "native" informant or interlocutor to authorize itself. He asks in this respect if, in effect, Rigoberta Menchú is not that, if the personal assumptions we bring to reading a testimonio are also those by which Latinamericanism seeks to define and appropriate its Other, and if, therefore, the promotion of testimonio by critics such as George Yúdice, Doris Sommer, or myself is not still "residually, but significantly, caught up in a certain representational strategy, which they themselves claim to have overcome."[7] I believe Elzbieta Sklodowska has in mind something similar when she claims that, despite its appeal to the authority of an actual subaltern voice, testimonio does not in fact represent "a genuine and spontaneous reaction of a 'multiform-popular subject' in conditions of postcoloniality, but rather continues to be a discourse of elites committed to the cause of democratization."[8] The appeal to authenticity and victimization in the critical validation of testimonio stops the semiotic play of the text, she seems to imply, fixing the subject in a unidirectional gaze that deprives it of its reality.[9]

At the same time, the deconstructive appeal to the "many-leveled, unfixable intricacy and openness of a work of literature"—the phrase is Spivak's but I think it captures Sklodowska's position on testimonio—itself has to be suspect, given that this "openness" happens in literature only in a structural relation in which literature itself is one of the social practices that generate the difference that is registered as subalternity in the testimonial text.[10] The limit of deconstruction in relation to testimonio is that it produces (or reveals) a textual unfixity or indeterminacy that not only misrepresents—in the sense both of "speaking for" and "speaking about"[11]—but itself produces and reproduces as a reading effect the fixity of relations of power and exploitation in the real social "text." The danger is that by being admitted into the academic canon, as in the course on Cultures, Ideas, and Values developed by Renato Rosaldo and Mary Louise Pratt to meet the undergraduate requirement in Western culture at Stanford, Rigoberta Menchú becomes simply a Clintonesque variant of Richard Rodriguez, yet another subaltern reprocessed into the hegemony by Stanford, which specializes in that sort of thing (*Hunger of Memory* hinges on Rodriguez's experience as an undergraduate "scholarship boy" at Stanford).

Is testimonio, as Sklodowska and, by implication, Moreiras suggest, simply another chapter in the history of what Ángel Rama called the "lettered city" in Latin America: the assumption, tied directly to the class interests of the Creole elites and their own forms of self-authorization, that literature and literary intellectuals—*letrados*—and the urban public sphere they define, are or could be adequate signifiers of the national?[12] The question is relevant to the claim made by Dinesh D'Souza in the debate over the Stanford Western culture curriculum that *I, Rigoberta Menchú* is not good or great literature. D'Souza wrote, to be precise: "To celebrate the works of the oppressed, apart from the standard of merit by which other art and history and literature is judged, is to romanticize their suffering, to pretend that it is naturally creative, and to give it an esthetic status that is not shared or appreciated by those who actually endure the oppression."[13] To my mind, *I, Rigoberta Menchú* is one of the most interesting works of *literature* produced in Latin America in the last fifteen years; but I would rather have it be a provocation in the academy, a radical otherness, as D'Souza feels it to be, than something smoothly integrated into a curriculum for "multicultural" citizenship of an elite university. I would like—and this was also Pratt and Rosaldo's aim—students at Stanford, or, for that matter, at the University of Pittsburgh, where I teach (although the contexts in class terms are somewhat different) to feel uncomfortable rather than virtuous when they read a text like *I, Rigoberta Menchú*. I would like them to understand that almost by definition the subaltern, which will in some cases intersect with aspects of their own personal identity, is not, and cannot be, adequately represented in literature or in the university, that literature and the university are among the institutional practices that *create* and sustain subalternity.[14]

I recognize that there are problems with such a stance, beginning with the fact that I myself have taught *I, Rigoberta Menchú* at, among other places, Stanford. I am not claiming, therefore, to have some specially privileged, politically correct stance on testimonio. In fact, I am beginning to think that the idea of testimonio as a kind of antiliterature I expressed in my first essays on the form such as "The Margin at the Center" may well neglect the fact that the Althusserian idea of "theoretical antihumanism" on which it is based is passing, for all practical purposes, from leftist professors like myself to pragmatic administrators concerned with downsizing and adapting the traditional humanities curriculum to suit the emerging requirements of economic globalization, with its new emphasis on media, communications, and cybernetics. Menchú herself makes a point, in the interview with Brittin and Dworkin, of defending what she explicitly calls "humanism," seeing its destruction or attenuation as a cultural effect of capitalism: "No perder el humanismo porque ¿qué es lo que está dañando a mucha humanidad hoy por hoy? Que mucha gente ha perdido el humanismo" (Not to lose humanism because, what is it that's hurting a lot of people today? The fact that they've lost humanism).[15]

By the same token, the question of literature and "great books," or what gets taught as such, is not one that is easily dismissed. There is an important political and cultural point to be made, for example, by answering Saul Bellow's question (which I paraphrase) "Who is the Tolstoy of the Zulus? The Proust of the Papuans?" with the names of Ousmane Sembene or Ngugi wa Thiong'o, who are entitled to ask in reply what has Bellow written lately that is all that great?. I take it that something like this is what Edward Said has in mind in *Culture and Imperialism,* where he sees the Great Tradition of the European novel as being detached from its complicity with colonialism and assimilated and transformed by non-European writers like Sembene and Ngugi in the process of decolonization.[16] Ángel Rama's notion of "narrative transculturation" in Latin American fiction pointed in a similar direction.

But where Said envisions a new type of intellectual capable of producing in literature what he calls "a new way of telling," which would embody a sense of subaltern agency, part of the force of a testimonio like *I, Rigoberta Menchú* is to displace the centrality of intellectuals, and what they recognize as culture—including literature. Menchú is an intellectual too, but Said has in mind more a postcolonial version of what Gramsci called a traditional intellectual, that is, someone who meets the standards and carries the authority of high culture. By contrast, the concern with the question of subaltern agency in testimonio depends epistemologically on the strategy of what Ranajit Guha has called "writing in reverse," founded on the radical suspicion that intellectuals and writing practices are themselves complicit in maintaining relations of domination and subalternity.[17]

Along with my reservations about the idea of literary transculturation of the colonial or postcolonial subaltern *from above* (as Said and Rama suggest), however, I think it is also important to admit the counter-possibility of transculturation *from below*: in this case, for example, to worry less about how *we* appropriate Menchú, and to understand and appreciate more how she appropriates *us* for her purposes. This is a key theme in both *I, Rigoberta Menchú* (see, for example, the sections on how the Mayas use the Bible and Christianity, or why Menchú decides to learn Spanish), and in Menchú's interview with Brittin and Dworkin, where, among other things, she talks about the appropriation of modern science and technology by indigenous communities in the Americas.[18]

Sklodowska is right to point out that the voice in testimonio is a textual construct, and that we should beware of a metaphysics of presence perhaps even more here, where the convention of fictionality has been suspended, than in other areas. Since the Real is that which resists symbolization, it is also that which collapses the claim of any particular form of cultural expression to representational adequacy and value. As such, the Real is, like the subaltern itself, with which it is connected both conceptually and "really," not an ontological category but a relational one, historically, socially, psychically specific. Just as there are different strokes for different folks, we might say there are different Reals for different Symbolics. As subjects, our (non)access to the Real is necessarily through the Symbolic. Jean-Paul Sartre asked in his book on anti-Semitism what it would take to make someone give up anti-Semitism, since the very structure of prejudice guarantees that the only empirical evidence it will allow to consciousness is that which always-already confirms the prejudice. The answer is something like being trapped with the Other in an elevator that has broken down for several hours, that is, in a "limit-situation"—to use Sartre's own language—that involves an involuntary breakdown of ego boundaries.[19]

That would be an experience of the Real, as is, via the experience of the transference, psychoanalysis, which undoes the structure of neurosis or trauma. The picaresque novel in sixteenth-century Spain and Europe offered (the simulacrum of) an experience of the Real vis-à-vis the idealistic genre conventions of pastoral and chivalric romances. But a picaresque novel like the anonymous *Lazarillo de Tormes* (1554)—perhaps the first modern novel in European literature—isn't really "realistic": it is *too* sordid, too centered on elementary bodily processes and on the elaborate tricks the *picaro* has to play on his masters to get something to eat—more a kind of grotesque inversion of the genre conventions and devices of the novels of chivalry than a plausible representation of even the lower depths of the society of its day. Bakhtin made the same sort of claim for the role of the "dual-tone" and comic debunking in his study of Rabelais.

On the other hand, the Real is not the same thing as the concept we are perhaps more comfortable with, the "reality effect," as it is used in Barthesian or Althusserian criticism. When Lazarillo is beaten or the blind man crashes against the stone post, they are experiencing the Real, not a reality effect. In that sense, and here Sklodowska and I might find common ground, the Real, at least in its effects, is not too different from what the Russian Formalists called *ostranenie* or defamiliarization. Perhaps intending the pun with the French *touché,* Lacan himself uses the Aristotelian category of *tuché* or "fortune" to describe the (sudden, fortuitous) "encounter with the Real," as he puts it: the knock on the door that interrupts our dream (either as outside the dream or as another experience *in* it), or the piece of gum or dog shit that sticks to the sole of our shoe, resisting all attempts to dislodge it.[20]

Something of the experience of the body in pain or hunger or danger inheres in testimonio. That is certainly the sense of that extraordinary passage in *I, Rigoberta Menchú* where Menchú narrates the torture and execution of her brother by the army in the town plaza of Chajul. At the climax of the massacre, she describes how the witnesses experience an almost involuntary shudder of revulsion and anger, which the soldiers sense and which puts them on their guard.[21] Reading this passage, you also experience this revulsion, and possibility of defiance even in the face of the threat of death, through a mechanism of identification, just as you do at the most intense moments in *Schindler's List*—for example, when the women in the concentration camp, who have been congratulating each other on surviving the selection process, suddenly realize that their children have been rounded up in their absence and are being taken to the gas chambers in trucks. These are instances of *tuché,* places where the experience of the Real breaks through the repetitious passivity of witnessing imposed by the repression itself. By contrast, romanticizing victimization would in fact confirm the Christian narrative of suffering and redemption that underlies colonial or imperialist domination in the first place and that leads in practice more to a moralistic posture of guilty, benevolent paternalism than effective solidarity, which presumes an equality between the parties involved.[22]

The narration of the death of Menchú's brother is, as it happens, precisely the passage in *I, Rigoberta Menchú* whose literal veracity the anthropologist David Stoll has contested, claiming on the basis of his own interviews in the area Menchú comes from (where he spent several years doing field research) that the torture and massacre of her brother by the army happened in a different way, that Menchú could not have been an eyewitness to it, and that therefore her description is, in his words, "a literary invention."[23] Stoll has not chosen to press this charge, and Menchú has categorically denied it (no one, in any case, questions the fact itself of the torture and murder of the brother by a unit of the Guatemalan army); but he has retained the implication that Menchú is not a reliable narrator, that her transformation into something like a secular saint of the struggles of Guatemalan indigenous communities is unwarranted.[24]

Let me attempt a reply to Stoll's and similar reservations about the representativity of Menchú's account via an episode in Shoshana Felman and Dori Laub's book on testimonial representations of the Holocaust, which is connected to my mention of *Schindler's List* earlier. It has to do with the case of a woman survivor and the eyewitness account of the Auschwitz uprising she gave for the Video Archive for Holocaust Testimonies at Yale. At one point in her narrative, the survivor recalls that in the course of the uprising, in her own words, "All of a sudden, we saw four chimneys going up in flames, exploding. The flames shot into the sky, people were running. It was unbelievable."[25] Months later, at a conference on the Holocaust that featured a viewing of the videotape of the woman's testimony, this sequence became the focus of a debate. Some historians of the Holocaust who saw the video of the woman's testimony pointed out that only *one* chimney had been destroyed in the uprising, and that the woman had not mentioned in her account the fact that the Polish underground had betrayed the uprising. Given that the narrator was wrong about these crucial details, they argued, it might be best to set aside her whole testimony, rather than potentially give credence to the revisionists, who want to deny the reality of the Holocaust altogether by questioning the reliability of the factual record.

Laub and Felman note that, on that occasion,

> A psychoanalyst, who had been one of the interviewers of the woman, profoundly disagreed. "The woman was testifying," he insisted, "not to the number of the chimneys blown up, but to something else more radical, more crucial: the reality of an unimaginable occurrence. One chimney blown up at Auschwitz was as incredible as four. The number mattered less than the fact of the occurrence. . . . The woman testified to an event that broke the all compelling frame of Auschwitz, where Jewish armed revolts just did not happen, and had no place. She testified to the breakage of a framework. That was historical truth. (60)

The psychoanalyst was Laub, who goes on to explain:

> In the process of the testimony to a trauma, as in psychoanalytic practice, in effect, you often do not want to know anything except what the patient tells you, because what is important in the situation is the *discovery* of knowledge—its evolution, and its very *happening*. Knowledge in the testimony is, in other words, not simply a factual given that is reproduced and replicated by the testifier, but a genuine advent, an event in its own right. . . . [The woman] was testifying not simply to empirical historical facts, but to the very secret of survival and of resistance to extermination. The historians could not hear, I thought, the way in which her silence was itself part of the testimony, an essential part of the historical truth she was precisely bearing witness to. . . . This was her way of being, of surviving, of resisting. It is not merely her speech, but the very boundaries of silence which surround it, which attest, today as well as in the past, to this assertion of resistance. (62)

I have argued elsewhere that it would be yet another version of the "native informant" of classical anthropology to grant testimonial narrators like Rigoberta Menchú only the possibility of being witnesses, but not the power to create their own narrative authority and negotiate its conditions of truth and representativity. "That would be a way of saying that the subaltern can of course speak, but only through the institutionally sanctioned authority—itself dependent on and implicated in colonialism and imperialism—of the journalist or ethnographer, who alone has the power to decide what counts in the narrator's 'raw material' and to turn it into literature (or 'evidence')."[26]

It is not incidental that Stoll relates his doubts about the veracity of *I, Rigoberta Menchú* to an uneasiness with what he calls explicitly "postmodernist" anthropology: "What I want to say," he notes, "is that if our frame is the text, the narrative, or the voice instead of the society, culture, or political economy, it is easy to find someone to say what we want to hear" (Stoll 1990, 11). But his own basis for questioning Menchú's account are interviews years later with people from the village where the massacre occurred; that is, the only thing he can put in the place of what he considers Menchú's inadequately representative testimony are other testimonies: other texts, narratives, versions, and voices.

We know something about the nature of this problem. There is not, outside of discourse, a level of social facticity that can guarantee the truth of this or that representation, given that what we call "society" itself is not an essence prior to representation but precisely the consequence of struggles to represent and over representation.[27] That is the deeper meaning of Walter Benjamin's aphorism "Even the dead are not safe": even the memory of the past is conjunctural, relative, perishable, dependent on practice. Testimonio is both an art and a strategy of subaltern memory.

Since Stoll raises directly the question of the authority of conventional anthropology against what is, for him, its corruption by the postmodern kind, let me say a few words about the relation of Menchú to Mayan tradition. In a sense, though it is founded on a notion of the authority of tradition, there is nothing particularly traditional about Menchú's narrative: this is not what makes it, as she claims, the expression of "toda la realidad de un pueblo" (the whole reality of a people), because there is nothing particularly traditional about the community and way of life that her testimonio describes either. Nothing more "postmodern," nothing more traversed by the economic and cultural forces of transnational capitalism—nothing that Stoll or, for that matter, we can claim anyway—than the social, economic, and cultural contingencies Menchú and her family live and die in. Even the communal mountain *aldea* or village that the text evokes so compellingly, with its collective rituals and economic life that make it seem like an ancestral Mayan gemeinschaft that has survived five hundred years of conquest more or less intact, turns out on closer inspection to be a recent settlement, founded by Menchú's father, Vicente, on unoccupied lands in the mountains in the wake of its inhabitants' dispossession by landowners from their previous places of residence, much as squatters from the countryside have created the great slums around Latin American cities, or returned refugees in Central America have tried to reconstruct their former communities.[28]

I do not mean by this to diminish the force of Menchú's insistent appeal to the authority of her ancestors or of tradition, but want simply to indicate that it is an appeal that is being activated *in the present*, that it is a response to the conditions of proletarianization and semiproletarianization that subjects like Menchú and her family are experiencing in the context of the *same* processes of globalization that affect our own lives. In some ways, Latin American cultural studies theorists such as Néstor García Canclini or Carlos Monsiváis, or postmodernist performance artists such as Gloria Anzaldúa or Guillermo Gómez Peña, might be better guides to Menchú's world than anthropologists such as David Stoll or Elisabeth Burgos, who, whatever their differences about the truth-value of Menchú's narrative, assume they are authorized or authorize themselves to represent that world for us. We all remember, in particular, Burgos's description (which I'm sure she now bitterly regrets) of Menchú's indian clothing ("She was wearing traditional costume, including a multicoloured *huipil* with rich and varied embroidery . . .") in her preface to *I, Rigoberta Menchú*, and probably tend to see this as an example of the self-interested benevolence of the hegemonic intellectual toward the subaltern. But Menchú's outfit is not so much an index of her authenticity as a subaltern, which would confirm the ethical and epistemological virtue of the *bien-pensant* intellectual in the First World—both as a field-worker in the huge agro-export coastal plantations of Guatemala and later as a maid in Guatemala City she had to learn how to dress very differently, as she tells us herself. It speaks rather to a kind of "performative" transvestism on her part, a conscious use of traditional Mayan women's dress as a cultural signifier to define her own identity and her allegiance to the community and values she is fighting for. Menchú notes in her narrative, for example, that "In the eyes of the community, the fact that anyone should even change the way they dress shows a lack of dignity. Anyone who doesn't dress as our grandfathers, our ancestors, dressed, is on the road to ruin" (37). At the same time, I am told by the Guatemalan novelist Arturo Arias, who has worked with her, that Menchú prefers blue jeans and T-shirts outside the public eye. There is a question of agency here, as in the construction of the testimonial text itself, and, as Menchú puts it in a phrase Brittin and Dworkin use as the subtitle of their interview, "los indígenas no nos quedamos como bichos aislados, inmunes, desde hace 500 años. No, nosotros hemos sido protagonistas de la historia" (We indians have not survived as strange, isolated beasts for five hundred years. No, we have also been protagonists of history) (Brittin and Dworkin, 212).

The Real that *I, Rigoberta Menchú* forces us to confront, in other words, is not only that of the subaltern as "represented" victim of history but also as agent of a transformative project that aspires to become hegemonic in its own right. For this project, testimonio is a means rather than an end in itself. As distinct from *Hunger of Memory*, becoming a writer, producing a literary text, cannot be the solution required by the "situation of urgency" that generates the telling of the testimonio in the first place, whether or not these things actually happen. Menchú is certainly aware that her testimonio can be an important tool in human rights and solidarity work that might have a positive effect on the genocidal conditions the text itself describes. But *her* interest in creating the text is not in the first place to have it become part of the canon of Western Civilization, which in any case she distrusts deeply, so that it can become an object *for us*, in a sense, our means of getting the "whole truth"—"toda la realidad"—of her experience. It is rather to act tactically in a way she hopes and expects will advance the interests of the community and social groups and classes her testimonio represents: "poor" Guatemalans. That is why *I, Rigoberta Menchú* can never be "great literature" in the sense that Dinesh D'Souza means this, because the response it elicits is something outside of the "field" of literature in its present form.[29]

The Real is supplementary in the Derridean sense, in that it indicates something that is in excess of the closure of representation. Asked by Brittin and Dworkin if she believes that her struggles will have an end, Menchú answers: "Yo sí creo que la lucha no tiene fin. . . . yo creo que la democracia no depende de una implantación de algo, sino que va a ser un proceso en desarrollo, se va a desenvolver a lo largo de la Historia" (I believe that the struggle does not have an end. . . . I believe that democracy does not depend on the implantation of something, but rather that it is a process in development, that it will unfold in the course of History) (213). She sees her own text in similar terms as a conjunctural intervention that responded to a certain strategic urgency, now relativized by what was not or could not be included in it—the imperfect metonym of a different, potentially more inclusive, and complete text. It is not so much that she is bothered, as we have often imagined, by Elisabeth Burgos's editing of the original transcript. Except for wanting to be recognized as the author, she doesn't complain about this. Her concern is elsewhere:

> Ahora, al leerlo, me da la impresión que es una parte, que son fragmentos de la historia misma, ¿verdad? Tantas anécdotas que uno tiene en la vida, especialmente la convivencia con los abuelos, con la familia, con la tierra, con muchas cosas. Son fragmentos los que tiene el libro y ojalá que algún día pudiéramos redocumentarlo para publicarlo, tal vez para nuestros nietos, posiblemente después de poner una serie de otras leyendas, testimonios, vivencias, creencias, oraciones, que aprendimos de chiquitos, porque el libro tiene una serie de limitaciones. (217)

> Reading it now, I have the impression that it's a part, that these are fragments of history itself, no? So many stories one comes across in life, in our experiences with the family, with the land, with so many things. What the book has are fragments and I hope that one day we could redo it, maybe for our grandchildren, maybe after putting in a series of other stories, testimonies, experiences, beliefs, prayers that we learned as children, because the book has a lot of limitations.

Note that Menchú distinguishes in this passage between her text as *a* testimonio—the book *I, Rigoberta Menchú* ("Son fragmentos los que tiene el libro")—and *testimonios* in the plural as heterogeneous and primarily oral acts or practices of witnessing and recounting in her own community, as in "una serie de otras leyendas, testimonios, vivencias, creencias, oraciones . . ." Testimonio is for Menchú, in other words, only *one*, highly specialized and conjunctural, part of a much larger testimonial practice in subaltern culture, which includes the arts of oral memory, storytelling, gossip, and rumor: precisely the arts Rigoberta Menchú learns from her mother, whose own life she calls a "testimonio vivo," or living testimony.[30] It happens to be the part *we* get to see, via the intervention of an interlocutor who is in a position to make a print text out of it, but this is not to say that it is not somehow connected to that larger testimonial practice and the intentionalities that underlie it, that it is simply a new way of constructing the subaltern in literature by or for intellectuals, as Sklodowska argues.

It is useful to remember in this respect that the subaltern does not *want* to remain subaltern; it is not the intention of its cultural practices, particularly where these address an interlocutor from the hegemony, as in the case of *I, Rigoberta Menchú*, to simply signify its subalternity.

This is perhaps the best way to confront the circumstance that the moment of testimonio is over. Not, so that I am not misunderstood on this point, testimonio as such: that will go on, just as testimonial forms have been present at the margins of Western literature ever since its inception as a modern episteme in the sixteenth century. But testimonio's moment, the originality and urgency or—to use Lacan's phrase—the "state of emergency" that drove our fascination and critical engagement with it, has undoubtedly passed, if only by the logic of aesthetic familiarization. Testimonio began as an adjunct to armed liberation struggle in Latin America and elsewhere in the Third World in the 1960s. But its canonization was tied even more, perhaps, to the military, political, and economic force of counterrevolution in the years after 1973. It was the Real, the voice of the body in pain, of the disappeared, of the losers in the rush to marketize, that demystified the false utopian discourse of neoliberalism, its claim to have finally reconciled history and society. At the same time, testimonio relativized the leftist or progressive claim of the high-culture writers and artists of the Boom to speak for the majority of Latin Americans. It marked a new site of discursive authority, which challenged the authority of the "great writer" to establish the reality principle of Latin American culture and development.

Testimonio was intimately linked to international solidarity networks in support of revolutionary movements or struggles around human rights, apartheid, democratization; but it was also a way of testing the contradictions and limits of revolutionary and reformist projects still structured in part around elite assumptions about the role of cultural vanguards. Detached from these contexts, it loses its special aesthetic and ideological power, and runs the risk of becoming a new form of *costumbrismo*, the Spanish term for "local-color" writing.

In his essay on Domitila Barrios and her well-known testimonio about Bolivian mining communities, *Let Me Speak!*, Javier Sanjinés in a sense is writing the epitaph for testimonio.[31] Barrios had ended her narrative with the wish that the text of her story would find its way back into the mining communities it described, as a tool for consciousness-raising and struggle. That question, the way in which subaltern groups themselves appropriate and *use* testimonio, I have suggested here, has not been addressed adequately in the discussion that has gone on among ourselves in the metropolitan academy. Sanjinés, however, is concerned with a different problem altogether: the fact that these mining communities, like the gigantic steel mills of my own city, Pittsburgh, have been significantly reduced in size or have ceased to exist altogether as the shifts of the global economy in the last twenty years have undermined the viability of the tin-mining industry in Bolivia, and that new forms of proletarian and subproletarian life have begun to appear in their place.

His point is that testimonios like *Let Me Speak!* can no longer be considered an adequate representation of subalternity in relation to domination; that—along with much of the traditional left and trade-union movement—they have become a nostalgia; that new forms of political imagination and organization are needed; that, as in everything else in life, we have to move on. Although Menchú speaks of redoing *I, Rigoberta Menchú,* she also suggests in the interview with Brittin and Dworkin that simply returning to testimonio now is beside the point, for she has other things she needs or wants to do, which include writing conventionally literary poems in Spanish (the interview concludes with the text of one of these, "Patria abnegada"). In a way, that is as it should be, because it is not only *our* purposes that count in relation to testimonio.

Fredric Jameson speaks in his review article on the Routledge *Cultural Studies* reader of "the desire called Cultural Studies," describing that desire as "the project to constitute a 'historic bloc,' rather than theoretically, as the floor plan for a new discipline."[32] Could we ask similarly, What is left today of the desire called testimonio? There are many ways one could answer this question, but it might be enough to say simply, understanding that it has functioned politically as something like what Lacan meant by the Real, Chiapas.

(1996)

4
What Happens When the Subaltern Speaks: Rigoberta Menchú, Multiculturalism, and the Presumption of Equal Worth

In one of the most powerful sections of *I, Rigoberta Menchú*, Menchú narrates the torture and execution of her brother Petrocinio by elements of the Guatemalan army in the plaza of a small highland town called Chajul, which is the site of an annual pilgrimage by worshipers of the local saint. Here is part of her account:

> After he'd finished talking the officer ordered the squad to take away those who'd been "punished," naked and swollen as they were. They dragged them along, they could no longer walk. Dragged them to this place, where they lined them up all together within sight of everyone. The officer called to the worst of the criminals—the *Kaibiles*, who wear different clothes from other soldiers. They're the ones with the most training, the most power. Well, he called the *Kaibiles* and they poured petrol over each of the tortured. The captain said, "This isn't the last of their punishments, there's another one yet. This is what we've done with all the subversives we catch, because they have to die by violence. And if this doesn't teach you a lesson, this is what'll happen to you too. The problem is that the Indians let themselves be

led by the communists. Since no-one's told the Indians anything, they
go along with the communists." He was trying to convince the people
but at the same time he was insulting them by what he said. Anyway,
they [the soldiers] lined up the tortured and poured petrol on them;
and then the soldiers set fire to each one of them. Many of them begged
for mercy. Some of them screamed, many of them leapt but uttered
no sound—of course, that was because their breathing was cut off.
But—and to me this was incredible—many of the people had weapons
with them, the ones who'd been on their way to work had machetes,
others had nothing in their hands, but when they saw the army setting
fire to the victims, everyone wanted to strike back, to risk their lives
doing it, despite all the soldiers' arms. . . . Faced with its own cow-
ardice, the army itself realized that the whole people were prepared to
fight. You could see that even the children were enraged, but they didn't
know how to express their rage. . . . [T]he officer quickly gave the order
for the squad to withdraw. They all fell back holding their weapons up
and shouting slogans as if it were a celebration. They were happy! They
roared with laughter and cried "Long live the Fatherland! Long live
Guatemala! Long live our President! Long live the army!"[1]

Much of the force of this passage derives from the fact that it pretends
to be the account of a witness, that is, testimony in both the legal and the
evangelical sense. Menchú was there; she and her family traveled all night
over mountain paths to be in Chajul; like the writers of the Gospels, she
saw with her own eyes the terrible wounds on her brother's body, saw him
being burned alive, felt the surge of rage of the crowd against the *Kaibiles*.

"What if much of Rigoberta's story is not true?" David Stoll asks in
his book about *I, Rigoberta Menchú*.[2] On the basis of interviews in the
area where the massacre was supposed to have occurred, Stoll concludes
(63–70) that the killing of Menchú's brother did not happen in exactly
this way, that Menchú was not a direct witness to the event, as her account suggests, and that therefore this account, along with other details
of her *testimonio*, amounts to, in his words, a "mythic inflation" (232).

It would be more accurate to say that what Stoll has been able to show
is that *some* rather than "much" of Menchú's story is not true. It is important to distinguish this claim from the claim subsequently made by some
right-wing commentators that *I, Rigoberta Menchú* is fraudulent. Stoll is
not saying that Menchú is making it all up. He does not contest the fact
of the murder of Menchú's brother by the army. And he stipulates in his
preface that "[t]here is no doubt about the most important points [in her
story]: that a dictatorship massacred thousands of indigenous peasants,

that the victims included half of Rigoberta's immediate family, that she fled to Mexico to save her life, and that she joined a revolutionary movement to liberate her country" (viii). But he does argue that the inaccuracies, omissions, or misrepresentations he finds in her narrative make her less than a reliable representative of the interests and beliefs of the people she claims to be speaking for.

If (in my account of the form) *"testimonio* [is] a narrative . . . told in the first person by a narrator who is also the real protagonist or witness of the events he or she recounts,"[3] then (referring in part specifically to these remarks) Stoll argues that "[j]udging by such definitions, *I, Rigoberta Menchú* does not belong in the genre of which it is the most famous example, because it is not the eyewitness account it purports to be" (Stoll 242).

In response to Stoll's charges, Menchú has publicly conceded that she grafted elements of other people's experiences and stories onto her own account. In particular, she has admitted that she was not herself present at the massacre of her brother and his companions in Chajul, and that the account of the event quoted in part above came instead from her mother, who (she claims) was in fact there. She says that these interpolations were a way of making her story a collective account, rather than an autobiography.[4] I personally don't find this explanation (or the related idea that Mayan forms of storytelling merge the individual experience in the collective) entirely satisfactory. I think it would have been better for Menchú to have indicated when she was speaking from or about someone else's experience. But, of course, that would have diminished the force of direct witness that the account carries. And Menchú, who tells us in her testimonio that she was trained to be a catechist of the word *(catequista de la palabra)*—that is, someone charged with explaining biblical stories to the people of her community in a way they could understand in terms of their own language and experience—is far from being a naive narrator. She cannot fail to be aware at some level of the resonance between her description of the death of her brother at the hands of the *Kaibiles* and the biblical story of the crucifixion. Would the truth the crucifixion has for Christians be altered if it could be shown, for example, that Luke was not actually present at the event, or that the accounts in Matthew, Mark, and John differ in some crucial ways from his—assuming, of course, that Luke is one person, and not, as seems more likely, a palimpsest of different authors and revisions?

The argument between Menchú and Stoll is not so much about what really happened as it is about who has the authority to narrate. What seems to bother Stoll above all is that Menchú *has* an agenda. He wants her to be a "native informant," who will lend herself to *his* purposes (of information gathering and evaluation); but she is instead something like what Gramsci meant by an "organic intellectual," concerned with producing a text of "local history" (to borrow Florencia Mallon's term)—that is, with elaborating hegemony.

The basic idea of Gayatri Spivak's famous, but notoriously difficult, essay "Can the Subaltern Speak?" might be reformulated in this way: if the subaltern could speak—that is, speak in a way that really *mattered* to us, that we would feel compelled to listen to, then it would not be subaltern. Spivak is saying, in other words, that one of the things being subaltern means is not mattering, not being worth listening to. By contrast, Stoll's argument with Rigoberta Menchú is precisely with the way in which her book "matters." It concerns how the canonization of *I, Rigoberta Menchú* was used by teachers like myself or solidarity and human rights activists to mobilize international support for the Guatemalan armed struggle in the 1980s, long after (in Stoll's view) that movement had lost whatever support it may have initially enjoyed among the Mayan peasants that Menchú claims to speak for. The inaccuracies and omissions in Menchú's account lend themselves, Stoll feels, "to justify violence" (274). That issue—"how outsiders were using Rigoberta's story to justify continuing a war at the expense of peasants who did not support it" (241)—is the main problem for Stoll, rather than the inaccuracies or omissions themselves. By making Menchú's story seem "the story of all poor Guatemalans," *I, Rigoberta Menchú* misrepresented a more complex and ideologically contradictory situation among the indigenous peasants.

In one sense, of course, there is a coincidence between Spivak's concern with the production in metropolitan academic and theoretical discourse of a "domesticated Other" in "Can the Subaltern Speak?" and Stoll's concern with the conversion of Menchú into an icon of political correctness in order to sustain a vanguardist political strategy in Guatemala he thinks was profoundly flawed. In a way that seems to echo Spivak, Stoll notes that

> books like *I, Rigoberta Menchú* will be exalted because they tell academics what they want to hear. . . . What makes *I, Rigoberta Menchú* so attractive in universities is what makes it misleading about the struggle for survival in Guatemala. We think we are getting closer to understanding Guatemalan peasants when actually we are being borne away by the mystifications wrapped up in an iconic figure. (227)

But Stoll's argument is also explicitly *with* Spivak, as a representative of the very kind of "postmodern scholarship" that would privilege a text like *I, Rigoberta Menchú*.[5]

I will come back to this point. For the moment, it may be enough to note that where Spivak is concerned with the way in which elite representation effaces the effective presence of the subaltern, Stoll's case against Menchú is precisely that: a way of, so to speak, *resubalternizing* a narrative that aspired to (and achieved) hegemony.

Although Stoll talks a lot about "facts" and "verification," it turns out that he also has an ideological agenda. He believes that the attempt of the left to wage an armed struggle against the military dictatorship in Guatemala put the majority of the highland indian population "between two fires," in his own image, driven to support the guerrillas mainly by the ferocity of the army's counterinsurgency measures rather than by a belief in the justice or strategic necessity of armed struggle. By contrast, the narrative logic of *I, Rigoberta Menchú* suggests that the Guatemalan armed struggle grew *necessarily* out of the conditions of repression the indigenous communities faced in their attempts to hold the line against land seizures and exploitation by the army, paramilitary death squads, and rich landowners anxious to appropriate their lands and their labor. For Stoll to sustain his hypothesis, he has to impeach the force of Menchú's testimony.[6]

But is the problem for Stoll the verifiability of Menchú's story or the wisdom of armed struggle as such? Stoll's position is *political*, in a way that is not susceptible to factual proof, just as, say, being a Democrat or a Republican is a political-ideological rather than a rational-empirical choice. If it could be shown that all the details in Menchú's account were in fact verifiable, would it follow for Stoll that the armed struggle was justified? Obviously not. But, by the same token, the gaps, inaccuracies, "mythic inflation," and so on he finds in Menchú's account do not necessarily add up to an indictment of the armed struggle. It may well be that armed struggle was a mistake: Stoll observes that Menchú has sought in recent years to place some distance between herself and the umbrella organization of the revolutionary left, the UNRG (Unidad Nacional Revolucionaria Guatemalteca [Guatemalan National Revolutionary Unity]).[7] But that judgment does not in itself follow from his attempted impeachment of Menchú's narrative authority. In other words, the question of verifiability and representativity is subordinate to the question of Stoll's ideological disagreement with the strategy of armed struggle, which he claims *I, Rigoberta Menchú* is inextricably connected to.

In particular, it is a long way from saying, as Stoll does, that not *all* highland peasants supported the armed struggle, which is at best a truism, to claiming that the guerrilla movement lacked, or lost, any significant popular roots among them, that it was imposed on them against their will and interests. Stoll gives us no more "hard" evidence to support this contention than Menchú does to argue the contrary, and other close observers of the conflict, such as Carol A. Smith, have argued that the guerrillas were in fact relatively successful in recruiting the highland indigenous peasants to their cause, indeed, that the integration of the previously predominantly ladino guerrilla groups with significant elements of this population constituted a powerful challenge to the military dictatorship, that it was precisely that possibility that the army was seeking to destroy in the genocidal counterinsurgency war that Menchú describes in her narrative.[8] Who are we to believe? As in the impeachment trial of President Clinton, it comes down to a matter of "he said, she said," which in the last instance will be decided on *political* as well as epistemological grounds.

Moreover, one could certainly read *I, Rigoberta Menchú* as an indictment of the near-genocidal violence of the Guatemalan army and ruling class, without necessarily agreeing with the strategy of armed struggle (or with the particular way in which that strategy was carried out). I would argue that this is the way *I, Rigoberta Menchú* has been read, in fact, most often outside Guatemala: not so much as a celebration of guerrilla struggle (like, for example, Che Guevara's *Reminiscences of the Cuban Revolutionary War,* Omar Cabezas's *Fire from the Mountain,* or Mario Payeras's *Days of the Jungle*), but rather as a way of mobilizing international opinion in favor of an end to the violence (and also, as I elaborate on later, as a defense of indigenous cultural autonomy and identity politics, rather than left-wing revolutionary vanguardism). Referring to the tasks of the truth commissions established as part of the peace process in Guatemala, Stoll notes that "[i]f identifying crimes and breaking through regimes of denial has become a public imperative in peacemaking, if there is a public demand for establishing 'historical memory,' then *I, Rigoberta Menchú* cannot be enshrined as true in a way it is not" (273). Fair enough. But if the Guatemalan army had simply destroyed the guerrillas and imposed its will by force on the population, then there would have been no truth commissions in the first place. Yet Stoll faults Menchú's story among other things for helping guerrilla leaders "finally obtain the December 1996 peace agreement" (278). Does he think it would have been better *not* to have done this?

In the process of constructing her narrative and articulating herself as a political icon around its circulation, Menchú is becoming not-subaltern, in the sense that she is functioning as a subject of history. But the conditions of her becoming not-subaltern—her narrative choices, silences, "mythic inflation," "reinvention," and so on—entail necessarily that there are versions of "what really happened" that she does not or cannot represent without relativizing the authority of her own account. In any social situation—indeed, even within a given class or group identity—it is always possible to find a variety of narratives, points of view, that reflect contradictory agendas and interests. "Obviously," Stoll quite properly observes,

> Rigoberta is a legitimate Mayan voice. So are all the young Mayas who want to move to Los Angeles or Houston. So is the man with a large family who owns three worn-out acres and wants me to buy him a chain saw so he can cut down the last forest more quickly. Any of these people can be picked to make misleading generalizations about Mayas. (247)

The presence of "other" indigenous voices in Stoll's account makes Guatemalan indigenous communities—indeed, even Menchú's own immediate family—seem irremediably riven by internal rivalries, contradictions, different ways of telling.[9] But, in a way, this is to deny the possibility of political struggle as such, because a hegemonic project by definition points to a possibility of collective will and action that depends precisely on transforming the conditions of cultural and political disenfranchisement, alienation, and desperation that underlie these contradictions. The appeal to heterogeneity—"any of these people"—leaves intact the authority of the "outside" observer (that is, Stoll) who is alone in the position of being able to both hear and sort through the various testimonies. It also leaves intact the *existing* structures of political-military domination and cultural authority. The existence of "contradictions among the people"—for example, the interminable internecine fights over land and natural resource rights within and between peasant communities that Stoll puts so much emphasis on—does not deny the possibility of contradiction between "the people" as such (say, a worker-peasant-professional alliance of ladinos and indian poor peasants) and a dominant ethnic group, class, and state felt as deeply antagonistic and repressive. Yet Stoll seems uncomfortable with notions of class and ethnic conflict as such, as if to appeal to such notions were in itself to encourage the sort of politics he dislikes.

But, of course, Stoll's 's argument is not only about Guatemala. It is also with the discourses of multiculturalism and postmodernism in the North American academy, which he feels consciously or unconsciously colluded to perpetuate the armed struggle in Guatemala by promoting *I, Rigoberta Menchú* and making Menchú into an international icon. Thus, for example: "[i]t was in the name of multiculturalism that *I, Rigoberta Menchú* entered the university reading lists" (243). Or, "[u]nder the influence of postmodernism (which has undermined confidence in a single set of facts) and identity politics (which demands acceptance of claims to victimhood), scholars are increasingly hesitant to challenge certain kinds of rhetoric" (244). Or, "the identity needs of Rigoberta's academic constituency play into the weakness of rules of evidence in postmodern scholarship" (247). Or, "with postmodern critiques of representation and authority, many scholars are tempted to abandon the task of verification, especially when they construe the narrator as a victim worthy of their support" (274).

What starts off as a critique of the truth claims of Rigoberta Menchú's testimonio and the strategy of the Guatemalan guerrilla movement metamorphoses into an attack on what the neoconservative writer Roger Kimball memorably called "tenured radicals" in European and North American universities. The connection between postmodernism and multiculturalism that bothers Stoll is predicated on the fact that multiculturalism carries with it what Canadian philosopher Charles Taylor calls a "presumption of equal worth."[10] That presumption of equal worth implies a demand for epistemological relativism that coincides with the postmodernist critique of the Enlightenment paradigm. If there is no one universal standard for truth, then claims about truth are contextual: they have to do with how people construct different understandings of the world and historical memory from the same set of facts in situations of gender, ethnic, and class inequality, exploitation, and repression. As noted, the truth claims for a testimonial narrative like *I, Rigoberta Menchú* depend on conferring on the form a certain special kind of epistemological authority. But for Stoll this amounts to an idealization of the subaltern to favor the prejudices of a metropolitan academic audience, in the interest of a solidarity politics that (in his view) is doing more harm than good. Against the authority of testimonial "voice," Stoll wants to affirm the authority of the fact-gathering procedures of anthropology and journalism, in which testimonial accounts like Menchú's will be treated simply as raw material that must be processed by more objective techniques of assessment.

Homi Bhabha argues that, for Taylor, the presumption of equal worth "does not participate in the universal language of cultural value . . . for it focuses exclusively on recognition of the excluded." In other words, the presumption is not dictated by an ethical principle that exists prior to the claim of cultural recognition itself. Rather, it depends on what Taylor calls a "processual judgment" that involves working through cultural difference to arrive at a new "fusion of horizon" (Taylor's term). But, Bhabha counters, such

> working through cultural difference in order to be transformed by the other is not as straightforwardly open to the other as it sounds. For the

possibility of the "fusion of horizon" of standards—the *new* standard of judgement—is not all that new; it is founded on the notion of the dialogic subject of culture that we had *precisely at the beginning* of the whole argument. . . . that makes the fusing of horizons a largely consensual and homogenizing norm of cultural value or worth, based on the notion that cultural difference is fundamentally synchronous.[11]

What is clear in Bhabha's point about the nonsynchronicity of difference is that it is not an abstract legal, ethical, or epistemological principle that drives the "presumption of equal worth": it is rather the *specific* character of the various relations of subordination, exploitation, and marginalization produced by capitalist modernity itself, involving as they do at all moments racism, Eurocentrism, colonialism and its aftermath, the destruction or displacement of native populations and territorialities, demographic catastrophe and waves of mass immigration, combined and uneven development, boom and bust cycles, the imposition or perpetuation of patriarchal forms of authority and women's inequality, and so on.

If Bhabha is right, the thrust of Taylor's argument is to recode multiculturalism within the possibilities offered by the existing institutional-ideological superstructure of globalized capital and liberal democracy, including the academy. But for Bhabha there is clearly something more corrosive in the principle of multiculturalism. Would it be possible to derive from multiculturalism a more radical consequence politically, given that what is expressed in the various forms of identity politics are relations of subordination, exploitation, and repression produced by the character of capitalist modernity itself? The question has to do in turn with the relation of multiculturalism to, under conditions of globalization, the cultural identity of the nation.

I, Rigoberta Menchú is, among other things, an argument for understanding Guatemala itself as a deeply multicultural and multilingual nation, in which indians like herself—who make up more than half of the population—deserve greater cultural and legal autonomy. Mario Roberto Morales's book *La articulación de las diferencias* (The articulation of differences) centers in particular on the "interethnic debate" that has accompanied the 1996 signing of the peace accords in Guatemala and their subsequent implementation.[12] Morales shares with David Stoll a preoccupation with the way in which *I, Rigoberta Menchú* has been canonized by multiculturalism and postcolonial and subaltern studies theory in the U.S. academy; but, unlike Stoll, he is more concerned with the effects of this *inside* Guatemala, which, he feels, are to legitimize the emergent discourse of separatist Mayan identity politics.

For Morales, what is at stake in the interethnic debate in Guatemala is the future of the country and the Central American region as a whole in the conjuncture formed by the defeat or stalemate of the project of the revolutionary left and the effects of globalization that the region is experiencing in the wake of that defeat and will continue to have to confront in the new millennium. His way of posing the problem stems from a double personal crisis: the crisis of the revolutionary left with which he had identified as a writer; the crisis of the traditional concept of the Latin American writer as a sort of literary Moses—a *conductor de pueblos*—who was uniquely charged with representing the national.[13]

The idea of a synergistic relation between literature and the processes of national development in a country like Guatemala found its most powerful expression in the 1960s and 1970s in Ángel Rama's concept of "narrative transculturation": *transculturación narrativa*.[14] Transculturation functioned for Rama (as for the Cuban ethnographer Fernando Ortíz, from whom Rama borrowed the concept) as a *teleology* of the national, not without moments of violent confrontation, cultural genocide and loss, desperation, adaptation, and tenacious resistance, but *necessary* in the final analysis for the formation of an inclusive national-popular culture. In relation to what came to be known as the "indian question," in particular, Rama believed that the only viable option for the indigenous peoples of the Americas was racial-cultural *mestizaje*, a *mestizaje* that his concept of transculturation both represented as an empirical social given and postulated as a normative model for intercultural relations.

Rama's idea of transculturation coincided with the heyday of dependency theory in Latin America. Transculturation would be, so to speak, the "cultural" correlative of the process of "delinking" and autonomous economic development the dependency economists were advocating. Both transculturation and dependency theory stressed the "underdeveloped" character of Latin American states—their inability to represent culturally and politically and to utilize productively all of the human and natural elements of the continent. But to articulate the indigenous, the regional, the anachronistic, the subaltern, the marginal as a problem of their *integration* by the nation-state—that is, in relation to the "incomplete project of modernity" (I am alluding, of course, to Habermas's well-known slogan)—does not open up a conceptual space to represent these as entities in their own right, with their own demands, values, cultural practices, and historical narratives (which may or may not coincide with the narrative of the formation and evolution of the state). In particular, Rama's insistence on transculturation prevented him from being able to anticipate the emergence in the 1980s of the so-called new social movements in

Latin America—one of whose main characteristics was that, unlike the political left in both its communist and reformist forms, they not only did not base themselves on a narrative of transculturation but also felt compelled many times to resist or negate the force of such a narrative.

A similar failure, in my opinion, afflicts Morales's analysis of Guatemalan cultural politics today. The principal achievement of *La articulación de las diferencias* is to free Central American cultural criticism from the limits of a purely literary or "high-culture" concept of cultural agency. In its pages, we can see the cultural life of Guatemala as a heterotopic or "mixed space" in which the agendas of international NGOs and human rights organizations, the novels of Miguel Ángel Asturias and testimonios based on the authority of oral culture such as *I, Rigoberta Menchú*, the Tex-Mex songs of Selena broadcast from stations in the United States, and twenty-two (or more) distinct indigenous groups—each with its own language and cultural forms and practices—coexist. But something also survives in Morales's argument of Rama's idea of transculturation, albeit now expressed in a postmodernist idiom of "cultural studies" and "hybridity" (*La articulación de las diferencias* could be read as a Guatemalan version of Néstor García Canclini's *Hybrid Cultures*).

Although he concedes that Mayan identity politics is born out of conditions of extreme poverty and oppression, Morales feels that at best the discourse of cultural identity proposes a negotiation between indigenous cultural (and economic) elites with the Guatemalan state and globalization, and their insertion in both. In this sense, he argues (like Stoll about *I, Rigoberta Menchú*) that this discourse (1) does not represent—in the sense of speaking *about*: that is, mimetically—the life-world of Guatemalan indigenous peoples in their multiple accommodations and negotiations with both the surrounding ladino world and globalized or transnational cultural flows and products; and (2) does not represent—in the sense of speaking *for*: that is, politically—the possibility of what he calls an "interethnic alliance" capable of displacing the hegemony in Guatemala of groups espousing a neoliberal model of development and the continuing power of elements connected to the old military-oligarchic state.

Against the sharp indigenous/ladino binary in the discourse of Mayan identity politics, Morales defends in his book a process of what he calls *mestizaje cultural*—cultural mixture. Morales wants to mean by *mestizaje cultural* not so much the sublation of cultural difference in favor of the emergence of a common or shared national identity, as in the idea of *mestizaje* in earlier Latin American cultural thinking (in, for example, Vasconcelos or Martí), but rather a complex and permanent, never completely achieved, process of expression, negotiation, and hybridization of these differences. He recognizes the persistence of the multiethnic and multilinguistic character of the population of a country such as Guatemala, the justice of many of the demands of indigenous groups, even the desirability and practical possibility of semiautonomous indigenous regions within the "national" space of Guatemala.

But if, for Morales, both indigenous cultures and ladino culture participate in a common process of *mestizaje,* hybridization, and "negotiation," then the question is, What (or where) is their difference? Because there is, finally, a *difference* between indians and ladinos that the fact of racial-cultural *mestizaje* does not cancel, just as there are differences—antagonistic and nonantagonistic—of "identity," values, access to capital, power, or privilege between blacks and whites in the United States, or between men and women in all class societies. Morales's concern in attacking Mayan identity politics is nominally with the reconstruction of the project of the left in Guatemala after the defeat of the armed struggle. But a new form of the left that could become hegemonic cannot be founded on a notion of "hybridization" of differences. Rather, it is precisely (racial, ethnic, gender, class, etc.) "differences" that would potentialize a revised politics of the left as a *transformative* force. In other words, it is *from* multicultural difference that the possibility of reconstituting (or perhaps of constituting really for the first time) a genuinely popular bloc appears. (Morales sometimes indulges in an essentialism of his own, identifying multiculturalism with "Anglo" moralism and *mestizaje* with Latin America as such.)

What is important in identity politics is not so much the claim of cultural difference per se, which (as Morales properly notes) all too often can play into the hands of elites, and sustain or even widen existing power and economic differentials within subaltern or minority groups. But the "presumption of equal worth" that underlies these claims lends them a kind of communality in their very incommensurability. If multiculturalism is essentially a demand for equality of opportunity—in accord with the category of the subject and the principle of individual rights—then not only is it compatible with neoliberal hegemony but, in a sense, it actively requires the market and liberal democracy and legal categories to constitute itself as such. In turn, the logic of the state and corporate planning is to organize hybrid or heterogeneous populations into fixed identity categories: poor, black, gay, indigenous, Latino, woman, person with AIDS, Catholic, and so on. (Part of the problem with identity politics is, of course, that one person can be all these things at once.)

But if the demand is not so much for formal equality—the "level playing field"—as for *actual* epistemological, cultural, economic, and civic-political equality and self-realization, such that cultural difference (say, the fact of being a non-Spanish speaker in Guatemala) does not imply a limitation on citizenship, then the logic of multiculturalism will necessarily have to question the existing forms of cultural and political hegemony. To paraphrase a well-known argument of Ernesto Laclau and Chantal Mouffe: multiculturalism conforms to liberal pluralism because the identities in play in multiculturalism find in themselves the principle of their validity and rationality, rather than in a transcendental social principle or goal. On the other hand, to the extent that the auto-constitution of multicultural identities is tied to forms of subalternity, identity claims participate in a common "egalitarian imaginary"—as Laclau and Mouffe call it—that is potentially subversive of the existing order of things. What fuels identity politics, in other words, is hatred and negation of social inequality and discrimination *as such*. Even the trope of simple inversion—the first shall be last and the last first, "we have been naught, we shall be all"—that is the driving force of subaltern agency has at its core a displaced form of egalitarian imaginary (for if the relation of master and slave can be reversed, then these are simply "roles" and not ontological destinies).

This makes it possible to produce from identity politics not only the essentialism and separatism Morales is concerned about (in their most negative form, as ethnic cleansing), but also what Laclau and Mouffe call a "popular subject position"—that is, a position that divides the political-cultural space of the nation into two antagonistic blocs: the bloc of "the people" and the bloc of the elite or ruling class. The idea inherent in this argument is that one can derive a form of popular-democratic hegemony from the principle of multiculturalism. In other words, the "egalitarian imaginary" is a *necessary* rather than a contingent aspect of popular-democratic identity. "The people" is "essentially" multicultural (in the sense that Spivak intends in her concept of "strategic essentialism").

This is something quite different from generalizing the principle of heterogeneity to the whole social space, such that economic, racial, class, and gender inequalities and differences are seen as coincident with civil society as such. This would be, as I argued earlier apropos of Stoll's critique of Menchú's representativity, a way of neutralizing the political force of multicultural (as well as class and gender) difference. Rather, multicultural heterogeneity is *internal* to the identity of the people, which in turn has to be articulated against that which it is not, what Laclau and Mouffe call its "constitutive outside." The reason I have given so much critical attention to Morales's defense of *mestizaje* is that the "constitutive outside" of "the people" would have to be in some sense the logic of acculturation or transculturation of capitalist modernity itself, a logic that seems coextensive with, rather than in opposition to, *mestizaje*.

To put this another way, the unity and mutual reciprocity of the— necessarily heterogeneous—elements of "the people" depends (as the idea of the Rainbow Coalition meant to symbolize) on a recognition of the inevitability and desirability of "contradictions among the people," without the need to resolve cultural difference and incommensurability into a transcendent or unitary cultural or political teleology. A potentially hegemonic articulation of multiculturalism would not seek to transcend differences and affectivities. In this sense, in order to form the interethnic ladino-indigenous-mestizo alliance of the sort Morales would like to see in Guatemala, a struggle against ladino hegemony and for the affirmation of the value of indian culture and identity may be necessary *in the first place,* because the "negotiation" of difference can only come as a response to a *demand*.[15]

If hybridity, *mestizaje,* transculturation, and the like are understood by Morales primarily as the field of this "negotiation" or—to use Bhabha's concept—of the "translation" of difference, then the dispute is merely terminological: hybrid or binary, transcultured or heterogeneous, shared or incommensurable—it is more or less the same. But one also suspects in the Morales's activation of these concepts against the force of Mayan identity politics the persistence of a form of class (bourgeois or petit bourgeois) and ethnic (ladino-*letrado*) *anxiety* about being displaced at the center of the national culture by a multiform subaltern popular subject (akin to what Jean-François Lyotard means by "the pagan"), an anxiety that works itself out in the desire to contain the protagonism of that subject within limits that are familiar and acceptable *for us.*

I have argued elsewhere that it would be yet another version of the "native informant" to grant a narrator such as Rigoberta Menchú only the possibility of being a witness, but not the power to create his or her own narrative authority and negotiate its conditions of truth and representativity. This would amount to saying that the subaltern can, of course, speak, but only through *us,* through our institutionally sanctioned authority and pretended objectivity as journalists or social scientists, which gives us the power to decide what counts as relevant and true in the narrator's "raw material." What *I, Rigoberta Menchú* forces us to confront is not someone who is being represented for us *as subaltern,* but rather an active agent of a transformative cultural and political project that aspires to become hegemonic in its own right: someone, in other words, who assumes the right to tell the story in the way she feels will be most effective in molding both national and international public opinion in support of the ideas and values she favors, which include a new kind of autonomy and authority for indigenous peoples.[16]

Stoll and Morales point in somewhat different directions politically, although both share a critique of the project of the Latin American revolutionary left as such and its relation with solidarity politics and multiculturalism in the United States. To the extent that they make that critique through a neutralization and containment of Menchú's own claim to authority, both of their books seem to me contemporary instances of what Ranajit Guha calls (apropos of the official histories and accounts of peasant rebellions in nineteenth-century India) "the prose of counterinsurgency": that is, texts that capture the fact of subaltern agency and insurgency essentially through the cultural assumptions and practices of the elites which that agency and insurgency are directed against.[17]

(2001)

Notes

Preface

1. I am using lowercase "indian" to refer to indigenous peoples of the Americas and capitalized "Indians" to refer to South Asians.

Introduction

1. Rigoberta Menchú, with Elisabeth Burgos-Debray, *I, Rigoberta Menchú: An Indian Woman in Guatemala*, trans. Ann Wright (London: Verso, 1984), 1; Domitila Barrios de Chungara, with Moema Viezzer, *Let Me Speak! Testimony of Domitila, a Woman of the Bolivian Mines*, trans. Victoria Ortiz (New York: Monthly Review Press, 1978), 19; Nawaal El Saadawi, *Woman at Point Zero*, trans. Sherif Hetata (London: Zed Books, 1983), 11.

2. Richard Rorty, "Solidarity or Objectivity?" in *Post-Analytic Philosophy*, ed. John Rajchman and Cornel West (New York: Columbia University Press, 1985), 3.

3. David Stoll, *Rigoberta Menchú and the Story of All Poor Guatemalans* (Boulder, Colo.: Westview Press, 1999).

4. Doris Sommer, "Las Casas's Lies and Other Language Games," in *The Rigoberta Menchú Controversy*, ed. Arturo Arias (Minneapolis: University of Minnesota Press, 2001), 237–50.

5. Victor D. Montejo, "Truth, Human Rights, and Representation: The Case of Rigoberta Menchú," in Arias, *The Rigoberta Menchú Controversy*, 390.

6. Claudia Ferman, "Textual Truth, Historical Truth, and Media Truth: Everybody Speaks about the Menchús," in Arias, *The Rigoberta Menchú Controversy*, 169 n. 11.

7. For readers who might find these claims excessive or demagogic, I suggest a look at David Brock, *Blinded by the Right: The Conscience of an Ex-Conservative* (New York: Crown, 2002), which details the author's own involvement in the right-wing misinformation campaigns of the Newt Gingrich era. Also: "Advocates of slavery scrutinized the writings of fugitive slaves for errors—any excuse to deny the slaves' depictions of the abuses they endured—and they sometimes charged that the true authors were abolitionists, not slaves" (Henry Louis Gates Jr., "The Fugitive," *New Yorker* [February 18 and 25, 2002]: 106).

8. David Stoll, letter to the editor, *LASA Forum* 33:4 (winter 2003): 21.

9. Alice Brittin and Kenya Dworkin, "Rigoberta Menchú: 'Los indígenas no nos quedamos como bichos aislados, inmunes, desde hace 500 años. No,

nosotros hemos sido protagonistas de la historia,'" *Nuevo Texto Crítico* 6:11 (1993): 212.

10. On this point, see Victoria Stanford, "From *I, Rigoberta Menchú* to the Commissioning of Truth: Maya Women and the Reshaping of Guatemalan History," *Cultural Critique* 47 (winter 2001): 16–53.

11. Michael Hardt and Antonio Negri, *Empire* (Cambridge and London: Harvard University Press, 2000). Subsequent references are given in the text.

12. "The encounter between South Asian subaltern studies and Latin American critiques of modernity and colonialism have one thing in common: their conception that subalternity is not only a question of social groups dominated by other social groups, but of the subalternity in the global order, in the interstate system analyzed by Guha and by Quijano. Dependency theory was clearly an early reaction to this problematic. This is no doubt a crucial and relevant point today, when coloniality of power and subalternity are being rearticulated in a postcolonial and postnational period controlled by transnational corporations and by the network society" (Walter Mignolo, "Coloniality of Power and Subalternity," in *The Latin American Subaltern Studies Reader*, ed. Ileana Rodríguez [Durham, N.C., and London: Duke University Press, 2001], 441).

13. Ranajit Guha, "Preface," in *Selected Subaltern Studies*, ed. Ranajit Guha and Gayatri Spivak (New York: Oxford University Press, 1988), 35.

14. Michael Hardt, "The Unfinished Democratic Project of Modernity," cited from author's manuscript.

15. "I use the term *Exodus* here to define mass defection from the State. . . . Exodus is the foundation of a Republic. The very idea of 'republic,' however, requires a taking leave of State judicature: if Republic, then no longer State. The political action of Exodus consists, therefore, in an *engaged withdrawal*. Only those who own a way of exit for themselves can do the founding; but, by the opposite token, only those who do the founding will succeed in finding the parting of the waters by which they will be able to leave Egypt" (Paolo Virno, "Virtuosity and Revolution: The Political Theory of Exodus," in *Radical Thought in Italy: A Potential Politics,* ed. Paolo Virno and Michael Hardt [Minneapolis: University of Minnesota Press, 1996], 196).

16. Otto Bauer, *The Question of Nationalities and Social Democracy,* ed. Ephraim J. Nimni, trans. Joseph O'Donnell (Minneapolis and London: University of Minnesota Press, 2000), xxvii. Hardt and Negri take up Bauer, noting "in the gentle intellectual climate of that 'return to Kant,' these professors, such as Otto Bauer, insisted on the necessity of considering nationality a fundamental element of modernization. In fact, they believed that from the confrontation between nationality (defined as community of character) and capitalist development (understood as society) there would emerge a dialectic that in its unfolding would eventually favor the proletariat. This program ignored the fact that the concept of the nation-state is not divisible but rather organic, not transcendental but transcendent, and even in its transcendence it is constructed to oppose every tendency on the part of the proletariat to reappropriate social spaces and social

wealth. . . . The authors celebrated the nation without wanting to pay the price of this celebration. Or better, they celebrated it while mystifying the destructive power of the concept of nation. Given this perspective, support for the imperialist projects and interimperialist war were really logical and inevitable positions for social-democratic reformism" (*Empire* 111–12). The identification of the position of Austro-Marxism with social imperialism is, I believe, historically incorrect. Hardt and Negri may be confusing Bauer with Kautsky, whose theory of the nation as a community of language was precisely, as we noted here, the one taken over by Lenin and the Bolsheviks. See, for example, Ephraim J. Nimni, *Marxism and Nationalism: Theoretical Origins of a Political Crisis* (London: Pluto Press, 1994).

17. Dipesh Chakrabarty, *Provincializing Europe: Postcolonial Thought and Historical Difference* (Princeton, N.J., and Oxford: Princeton University Press, 2000), 95.

18. "The bibliography on culture tends to assume that there is an intrinsic interest on the part of the hegemonic sectors to promote modernity and a fatal destiny on the part of the popular sectors that keeps them rooted in traditions. From this opposition, modernizers draw the moral that their interest in the advances and promises of history justifies their hegemonic position: meanwhile, the backwardness of the popular classes condemns them to subalternity. . . . [But] traditionalism is today a trend in many hegemonic social layers and can be combined with the modern, almost without conflict, when the exaltation of traditions is limited to culture, whereas modernization specializes in the social and the economic. It must now be asked in what sense and to what ends the popular sectors [also] adhere to modernity, search for it, and mix it with their traditions" (Néstor García Canclini, *Hybrid Cultures: Strategies for Entering and Leaving Modernity*, trans. Christopher L. Chiappari and Silvia L. López [Minneapolis: University of Minnesota Press, 1995], 146).

19. Originally in *The Political Unconscious*. For a later restatement, see, for example, Jameson's essay on the Soviet film director Tarkovsky, "On Soviet Magic Realism," in *The Geopolitical Aesthetic: Cinema and Space in the World System* (Bloomington: Indiana University Press, 1992).

20. Gayatri Spivak, *Death of a Discipline* (New York: Columbia University Press, 2003), 90, 92.

21. Luis Tapia, *La condición multisocietal* (La Paz, Bolivia: Muela del Diablo, 2002).

22. Mahmood Mamdani, remarks at the conference "Subaltern Studies at Large," Columbia University, November 2000; Aamir Mufti, ed., *Critical Secularism*, forthcoming as a special issue of *boundary 2* 31: 2 (summer 2004). Mufti in particular is engaged in trying to find modes of cultural identity that transcend the "national" division between Pakistan and India, Hindus and Muslims. Similarly, although in the context of the bitter polarization between Israeli Jews and Palestinians it may seem quixotic, to say the least, to raise again the sixties-era slogan of a secular binational state that was abandoned in favor of the

"two-state" solution, nevertheless there may be some point to doing this. That is because, whatever the form of autonomy conceded to a West Bank Palestinian state (and it is hard to imagine under current conditions that entity as anything other than a stunted neocolonial contrivance, somewhat on the model of Puerto Rico), there will still remain a large Palestinian Arab population within Israel itself (today one-fifth of all Israeli citizens are Arab; given present demographic trends, by the end of this century perhaps one-third to one-half will be). There is a debate about whether the situation of that population can be characterized as one of apartheid, but there is no doubt that Israeli Arabs will necessarily be second-class citizens in a state that defines itself essentially as a state of the Jewish people. We come back to Otto Bauer: Would it not be better for Israel to recognize itself as what it is in fact, a multicultural, multireligious, and, above all, multinational state? On the question of Islamic fundamentalism and the secular left, I have found useful Susan Buck-Morss, *Thinking Past Terror: Islamism and Critical Theory on the Left* (London: Verso, 2003), esp. 41–62.

1. The Margin at the Center

1. Roberto Fernández Retamar, *Caliban and Other Essays*, trans. Edward Baker (Minneapolis: University of Minnesota Press, 1989), 5–6.

2. See Gayatri Chakravorty Spivak, *In Other Worlds: Essays in Cultural Politics* (New York: Methuen, 1988); Fredric Jameson, "Third World Literature in the Era of Multinational Capitalism," *Social Text* 15 (1986): 65–88; Aijaz Ahmad, "Jameson's Rhetoric of Otherness and the 'National Allegory,'" *Social Text* 17 (1987): 3–27; and Jameson's rejoinder to Ahmad in the same issue of *Social Text*.

3. Raymond Williams, "The Writer: Commitment and Alignment," *Marxism Today* 24 (June 1980): 25.

4. I will touch on Barbara Foley's work later. Testimonio is difficult to classify according to standard bibliographic categories. To what section of a library or a bookstore does a testimonio belong? Under whose name is a testimonio to be listed in a card catalog or database? How should it be reviewed, as fiction or nonfiction?

5. Barbara Harlow, *Resistance Literature* (New York: Methuen, 1987). Harlow is more attentive than Spivak or Jameson to the ways in which the social transformations produced by liberation struggles also transform or problematize the institution and existing forms of narrative literature itself.

6. The definition of testimonio in the rules of the Casa de las Américas prize is as follows: "Testimonios must document some aspect of Latin American or Caribbean reality from a direct source. A direct source is understood as knowledge of the facts by the author or his or her compilation of narratives or evidence obtained from the individuals involved or qualified witnesses. In both cases reliable documentation, written or graphic, is indispensable. The form is at the author's discretion, but literary quality is also indispensable" (my translation). On the Latin American reception of *In Cold Blood*, see Ariel Dorfman, "La

última novela de Capote: ¿Un nuevo género literario?" *Anales de la Universidad de Chile* 124 (1966): 97–117, one of the first elaborations of testimonio as a distinct genre.

7. Lewis and Pozas were actually reviving a form that had been initiated in the 1930s by University of Chicago anthropologists and had then fallen into disuse during the period of academic McCarthyism during the Cold War.

8. Thus there are Palestinian, Angolan, Vietnamese, Irish, Brazilian, South African, Argentinian, Nicaraguan, and other testimonial literatures. On guerrilla testimonio, see Harlow, *Resistance Literature*; Juan Duchesne, "Las narraciones guerrilleras: configuración de un sujeto épico de nuevo tipo," in *Testimonio y literatura*, ed. René Jara and Hernán Vidal (Minneapolis: Institute for the Study of Ideologies and Literature, 1986), 137–85.

9. One of the most important protagonists of the testimonio has been the North American socialist-feminist poet Margaret Randall, who played a major role in developing the form in Cuba in the 1970s and then in Nicaragua after 1979, where she conducted a series of workshops to train people to collect their own experience and begin building a popular history written by themselves. She is the author of a handbook on how to make a testimonio: *Testimonios: A Guide to Oral History* (Toronto: Participatory Research Group, 1985). Her own testimonial work available in English includes *Cuban Women Now* (Toronto: Women's Press, 1974); *Doris Tijerino: Inside the Nicaraguan Revolution* (Vancouver: New Star, 1978); *Sandino's Daughters* (Vancouver: New Star, 1981); *Christians in the Nicaraguan Revolution* (Vancouver: New Star, 1983); *Risking a Somersault in the Air: Conversations with Nicaraguan Writers* (San Francisco: Solidarity, 1985); and *Women Brave in the Face of Danger* (Trumansberg, N.Y: Crossing, 1987).

10. The reception of testimonio thus has something to do with a revulsion for fiction and the fictive as such, with its "postmodern" estrangement.

11. Georg Lukács, *The Theory of the Novel*, trans. Anna Bostock (Cambridge: MIT Press, 1971).

12. See Hans Robert Jauss, "Ursprung und Bedeutung der Ichform im *Lazarillo de Tormes*," *Romanische Jahrbuch* 10 (1959): 297–300.

13. René Jara, "Prólogo," in Jara and Vidal, *Testimonio y literatura*, 2.

14. Rigoberta Menchú, with Elisabeth Burgos-Debray, *I, Rigoberta Menchú: An Indian Woman in Guatemala*, trans. Ann White (London: Verso, 1984), 1.

15. See Jameson's idea of a postbourgeois "collective subject, decentered but not schizophrenic . . . which emerges in certain forms of storytelling that can be found in the third-world literature, in testimonial literature, in gossip and rumors, and in things of this kind. It is storytelling that is neither personal in the modernist sense, nor depersonalized in the pathological sense of the schizophrenic text" (in Anders Stephanson, "Regarding Postmodernism: A Conversation with Fredric Jameson," *Social Text* 17 [1987]: 45).

16. Ricardo Pozas, *Juan the Chamula: An Ethnological Recreation of the Life of a Mexican Indian*, trans. Lysander Kemp (Berkeley: University of California

Press, 1962); Domitila Barrios de Chungara, with Moema Viezzer, *Let Me Speak! Testimony of Domitila, a Woman of the Bolivian Mines*, trans. Victoria Ortiz (New York: Monthly Review Press, 1978); Randall, *Doris Tijerino*.

17. The most dramatic instance of this affirmation of the self that I know of occurs in the Egyptian testimonial novel written by Nawal El Saadawi, *Woman at Point Zero*, trans. Sherif Hatata (London: Zed Books, 1983). The narrator is Firdaus, a young prostitute who is about to be executed for murdering her pimp. Her interlocutor is the Egyptian feminist writer Nawal El Saadawi, who was at the time working in the prison as a psychiatrist. Firdaus begins by addressing this person, who represents, albeit in benevolent form, the repressive power of both the state and the institution of literature, as follows: "Let me speak! Do not interrupt me! I have no time to listen to you. They are coming to take me at six o'clock this evening" (11). Barbara Harlow notes that El Saadawi was herself imprisoned by the Sadat regime for feminist activities some years later and wrote an account of her experience in *Memoirs from the Women's Prison* (*Resistance Literature*, 139–40).

18. A kind of antitestimonio, for example, is Richard Rodriguez's *Hunger of Memory* (Boston: D. R. Godine, 1981), which is precisely a bildungsroman of the access to English-language literacy—and thence to middle-class status—by a Chicano from a working-class background. Because one of its themes is opposition to official bilingualism, it has become a popular text for neoconservative initiatives in education. Paradoxically, it is also used frequently in English writing classes by persons who would otherwise probably not identify with neoconservatism to indoctrinate students into the ideology of "good writing."

19. See Miguel Barnet, "La novela-testimonio: Socioliteratura," in *La fuente viva* (Havana: Editorial Letras Cubanas, 1983), 12–42.

20. Omar Cabezas, *Fire from the Mountain*, trans. Kathleen Weaver (New York: Crown, 1985).

21. Eliana Rivero, "Testimonios y conversaciones como discurso literario: Cuba y Nicaragua," in *Literature and Contemporary Revolutionary Culture*, ed. Hernán Vidal (Minneapolis: Society for the Study of Contemporary Hispanic and Lusophone Revolutionary Literatures, 1984–85), 218–28. Cabezas recorded himself and edited the transcript, acting as his own interlocutor.

22. Testimonio in this sense is uniquely situated to represent the components of what Sandinista theoreticians Roger Burbach and Orlando Nuñéz have called the "Third Force" in their potential linkage with working-class issues and movements: that is, middle-class intellectuals and sections of the petite bourgeoisie; marginalized social sectors; and what have come to be known as "new social movements" (religious *comunidades de base*, feminist groups, ecology organizations, human rights groups, and so on) (*Fire in the Americas: Forging a Revolutionary Agenda* [London: Verso, 1987]).

23. Menchú, *I, Rigoberta Menchú*, xx–xxi.

24. K. Millet, "Framing the Narrative: The Dreams of Lucinda Nahuelhaul,"

in *Poética de la población marginal: Sensibilidades determinantes,* ed. James Romano (Minneapolis: Prisma Institute, 1987), 425, 427.

25. Menchú, *I, Rigoberta Menchú,* 247.

26. See Gayatri Chakravorty Spivak, "Can the Subaltern Speak?" in *Marxism and the Interpretation of Culture,* ed. Cary Nelson and Lawrence Grossberg (Urbana: University of Illinois Press, 1988), 271–313.

27. Elzbieta Sklodowska, "La forma testimonial y la novelística de Miguel Barnet," *Revista/Review Interamericana* 12:3 (1982): 379.

28. Jara, "Prólogo," 2.

29. This seems in particular the outcome of Roberto González Echevarría's influential discussion of Miguel Barnet's *Autobiography of a Runaway Slave,* "*Biografía de un cimmarón* and the Novel of the Cuban Revolution," in *The Voice of the Masters: Writing and Authority in Modern Latin American Literature* (Austin: University of Texas Press, 1985), 110–24.

30. Barbara Foley, *Telling the Truth: The Theory and Practice of Documentary Fiction* (Ithaca, N.Y: Cornell University Press, 1986).

31. I have perhaps overstated here the distinction between testimonio and autobiography. I am aware, for example, of the existence in slave narratives, certain forms of women's writing, and in working-class, black, Latino, and gay literature in the United States, of something that might be called "popular" autobiography, somewhere between autobiography as I characterize it here and testimonio as such. Moreover, in Latin American writing autobiography often has a direct political resonance. See Sylvia Molloy, "At Face Value: Autobiographical Writing in Spanish America," *Dispositio* 24–26 (1985): 1–18.

32. Sidonie Smith, "On Women's Autobiography," paper delivered at a conference on autobiography, Stanford University, April 1986.

33. See, for example, Spivak, *In Other Worlds,* 209ff.; see also her critique of poststructuralist notions of the subject in "Can the Subaltern Speak?"

34. Foley claims that the documentary novel "locates itself near the border between factual discourse and fictive discourse, *but does not propose an eradication of that border.* Rather, it purports to represent reality by means of agreed-upon conceptions of fictionality, while grafting onto its fictive pact some kind of additional claim to empirical validation" (*Telling the Truth,* 25; emphasis mine).

35. Jara, "Prólogo," 3.

36. See Barnet, "La novela-testimonio."

2. "Through All Things Modern"

1. Rigoberta Menchú, with Elisabeth Burgos-Debray, *I, Rigoberta Menchú: An Indian Woman in Guatemala,* trans. Ann Wright (London: Verso, 1984), 170–71.

2. John Beverley, "The Margin at the Center: On Testimonio (Testimonial Narrative)," *Modern Fiction Studies* 35: 1 (spring 1989): 11–28, a special issue titled *Narratives of Colonial Resistance* edited by Timothy Brennan.

3. "My name is Rigoberta Menchú. I am twenty-three years old. This is my testimony. I didn't learn it from a book, and I didn't learn it alone. I'd like to stress that it's not only *my* life, it's also the testimony of my people. It's hard for me to remember everything that's happened to me in my life since there have been many very bad times but, yes, moments of joy as well. The important thing is that what has happened to me has happened to many other people too: My story is the story of all poor Guatemalans. My personal experience is the reality of a whole people" (1).

4. Gayatri Chakravorty Spivak, "Can the Subaltern Speak?" in *Marxism and the Interpretation of Culture,* ed. Cary Nelson and Lawrence Grossberg (Urbana: University of Illinois Press, 1988), 278.

5. Doris Sommer, "No Secrets," in *The Real Thing: Testimonial Discourse and Latin America,* ed. Georg M. Gugelberger (Durham, N.C.: Duke University Press, 1996), 157.

6. Thus, for example, Allen Carey-Webb, who taught an undergraduate course on world literature at the University of Oregon based entirely on testimonios, notes of *I, Rigoberta Menchú:* "[It] is one of the most moving books I have ever read. It is the kind of a book that I feel I must pass on, that I must urge fellow teachers to use in their classes. . . . My students were immediately sympathetic to Menchú's story and were anxious to know more, to involve themselves. They asked questions about culture and history, about their own position in the world, and about the purposes and methods of education. Many saw in the society of the Guatemalan Indian attractive features they found lacking in their own lives, strong family relationships, community solidarity, an intimate relationship with nature, commitment to others and to one's beliefs" (Allen Carey-Webb, "Teaching Third World Auto/Biography: Testimonial Narrative in the Canon and Classroom," *Oregon English* 12:2 (fall 1990): 8.

7. See, respectively, Fredric Jameson, "Third World Literature in the Era of Multinational Capitalism," *Social Text* 15 (1986): 65–88, and his interview with Anders Stephanson, *Social Text* 17 (1987): 26–27; Barbara Harlow, *Resistance Literature* (New York: Methuen, 1987); Barbara Foley, *Telling the Truth: The Theory and Practice of Documentary Fiction* (Ithaca, N.Y.: Cornell University Press, 1986); Margaret Randall, *Testimonios: A Guide to Oral History* (Toronto: Participatory Research Group, 1985); George Yúdice, "Marginality and the Ethics of Survival," in *Universal Abandon: The Politics of Postmodernism,* ed. Andrew Ross (Minneapolis: University of Minnesota Press, 1988), 214–36; Juan Duchesne, "Las narraciones guerrilleras: configuración de un sujeto épico de nuevo tipo," in *Testimonio y literatura,* ed. René Jara and Hernán Vidal (Minneapolis: Institute for the Study of Ideologies and Literature, 1986), 137–85; Spivak, "Can the Subaltern Speak?" 271–313; and Elzbieta Sklodowska, "La forma testimonial y la novelística de Miguel Barnet," *Revista/Review Interamericana* 12:3 (1982): 368–80.

8. Roberto González Echevarría, *"Biografía de un cimarrón* and the Novel of

the Cuban Revolution," in *The Voice of the Masters: Writing and Authority in Modern Latin American Literature* (Austin: Univeresity of Texas Press, 1985), 110–24.

9. An instance of this ambivalence may be found in the definition of testimonio in the contest rules of the prestigious literary prizes of Cuba's Casa de las Américas (it was the decision of Casa de las Américas in 1971 to offer a prize in this category that put testimonio on the canonical map of Latin American literature in the first place): "Testimonios must document some aspect of Latin American or Caribbean reality from a direct source. A direct source is understood as knowledge of the facts by the author or his or her compilation of narratives or evidence obtained from the individuals involved or qualified witnesses. In both cases reliable documentation, written or graphic, is indispensable. The form is at the author's discretion, *but literary quality is also indispensable*" (my translation and emphasis). But is there a determination of "literary quality" that does not involve in turn an ideology of the literary? Against a modernist bias in favor of textual collage and/or editorial elaboration in the preparation of a testimonial text, one could argue that a direct, "unliterary" narrative might have both a higher ethical *and* aesthetic status.

10. See, for example, the remarks of the great Peruvian novelist José María Arguedas on the difficulty of reconciling in his own work an inherited Spanish-language model of "literariness" with the representation of the world of Quechua- or Aymara-speaking Andean peasants: "I wrote my first story in the most correct and 'literary' Spanish I could devise. I read the story to some of my writer friends in the capital, and they praised it. But I came to detest more and more those pages. No, what I wanted to describe—one could almost say denounce—wasn't like that at all, not the person, not the town, not the landscape. Under a false language a world appeared as invented, without marrow and without blood: a typically 'literary' world in which the word had consumed the work" (José María Arguedas, "La novela y el problema de la expresión literaria en el Perú," in *Obras completas* [Lima: Editorial Horizonte, 1983] 2:196; my translation). Arguedas's solution was to develop a novel in Spanish, based stylistically and thematically on the tension between Spanish and Quechua. By contrast, there is the well-known example of the Kenyan writer Ngugi Wa Thiong'o who, in 1977, after publishing a series of successful anticolonial novels in English, decided to write his novels, plays, and stories exclusively in his tribal language, Kikuyu. See his *Decolonising the Mind: The Politics of Language in African Literature* (Portsmouth, N.H.: Heinemann, 1987).

11. Ana Guadalupe Martínez, *Las cárceles clandestinas de El Salvador* (Mexico City: Casa El Salvador, 1979), 12–14; my translation and emphasis.

12. See Roque Dalton's *Miguel Mármol* (San José, Costa Rica: EDUCA, 1982), a reconstruction of the life of one of the founders of the Salvadoran Communist Party, and his own autobiographical novel of the guerrilla underground, *Pobrecito poeta que era yo* (San José, Costa Rica: EDUCA, 1976).

13. Walter Mignolo, "Literacy and Colonization: The New World Experience," in *1492–1992: Re/Discovering Colonial Writing (Hispanic Issues* vol. 4), ed. René Jara and Nicholas Spadaccini (Minneapolis: Prisma Institute, 1989), 67.

14. Mignolo similarly is careful to distinguish in the same essay the literacy of the colonial and neocolonial state from the contemporary literacy campaigns instituted, for example, by the Cuban and Nicaraguan revolutions based on the methods of Paolo Freire's "pedagogy of the oppressed," which he sees as a means of empowerment of the subaltern.

15. "The testimonial 'I' in these books neither presumes nor even invites us to identify with it. We are too foreign, and there is no pretense here of universal or essential human experience" (Sommer, "No Secrets," 146).

16. Gayatri Spivak, "On the Politics of the Subaltern," interview with Howard Winant in *Socialist Review* 90:3 (July–September 1990): 91. To anticipate the inevitable objections (see, e.g., Benita Parry, "Problems in Current Theories of Colonial Discourse," *Oxford Literary Review* 9:1–2 [1988]: 27–58): the subaltern, of course, speaks quite a lot, but not *to* Gayatri Spivak, so to speak. It is not to trivialize Che Guevara's example to observe that his eerily prophetic sense—noted in his *Bolivian Diary*—of the blankness in the eyes of the peasants he encountered in the course of trying to establish a guerrilla *foco* in the Bolivian Andes might have been otherwise had he been able to speak their language, Aymara.

17. On this point, see James Clifford, "On Collecting Art and Culture," in *Out There: Marginalization and Contemporary Culture,* ed. Russell Ferguson (Cambridge: MIT Press, 1990).

18. John Beverley and Marc Zimmerman, *Literature and Politics in the Central American Revolutions* (Austin: University of Texas Press, 1990).

19. Ángel Rama, *La ciudad letrada* (Hanover, N.H.: Ediciones del Norte, 1984).

20. China, the Indian subcontinent, and Islamic Africa had written literatures before colonialism, and in this sense differ from Latin America, which experienced a much deeper degree of European colonization both culturally and demographically. But I would argue that, whatever their links to the past, modern literatures in the Third World generally are also basically engendered by colonialism and imperialism.

21. See Rama, *La ciudad letrada*; and in particular Alejandro Losada, "La literatura urbana como praxis social en América Latina," *Ideologies and Literature* 1:4 (1977): 33–62.

22. Julio Ramos, *Desencuentros de la modernidad en América Latina: Literatura y política en el siglo XIX* (Mexico City: Fondo de Cultura Económica, 1990).

23. Sylvia Molloy, "From Serf to Self: The Autobiography of Juan Francisco Manzano," *Modern Language Notes* 104 (1989): 417.

24. Yúdice, "Marginality and the Ethics of Survival"; Neil Larsen, *Modern-*

ism and Hegemony: A Materialist Critique of Aesthetic Agencies (Minneapolis: University of Minnesota Press, 1989), xxxi.

25. I share Jameson's sense in the concluding remarks to his book on post-modernism that the concept, which has certainly been devoured by habitualiza-tion (and perhaps also by the current recession), is still worth using: "I occasion-ally get just as tired of the slogan 'postmodern' as anyone else, but when I am tempted to regret my complicity with it, to deplore its misuses and its notoriety, and to conclude with some reluctance that it raises more questions than it solves, I find myself pausing to wonder whether any other concept can dramatize the issues in quite so effective and economical a fashion" (Fredric Jameson, *Post-modernism, or, The Cultural Logic of Late Capitalism* [Durham, N.C.: Duke University Press, 1990], 410).

26. See, for example, Yúdice's "Marginality and the Ethics of Survival."

27. On this point, I find myself in sharp disagreement with Neil Larsen's Leninist "critique of aesthetic agencies" in *Modernism and Hegemony*, which I think has in common with a social-democratic counterpart like Habermas's both the discomfort of what Gramsci called the "traditional intellectual" in the face of the emergence of mass culture and a corresponding nostalgia for a "rational" politics of clearly class-based parties.

3. The Real Thing

1. "The *Ding* is not in the relationship—which is to some extent a calculated one insofar as it is explicable—that causes man to question his words as referring to things which they have moreover created. There is something different in *das Ding*. . . . If Freud speaks of the reality principle, it is in order to reveal to us that from a certain point of view it is always defeated; it only manages to affirm itself at the margin. And this is so by reason of a kind of pressure that . . . Freud calls not 'the vital needs'—as is often said in order to emphasize the secondary processes— but *die Not des Lebens* in the German text. An infinitely stronger phrase. Some-thing [some thing] that *wishes*. 'Need' and not 'needs.' Pressure, urgency. The state of *Not* is the state of emergency in life. . . . As soon as we try to articulate the reality principle so as to make it depend on the physical world to which Freud's purpose seems to require us to relate it, it is clear that it functions, in fact, to isolate the subject from reality" (Jacques Lacan, *The Seminar of Jacques Lacan. Book VIII. The Ethics of Psychoanalysis* [New York: Norton, 1993], 46).

2. Slavoj Žižek, "From Courtly Love to *The Crying Game*," *New Left Re-view* 202 (1993): 96. Žižek's remarks follow on Lacan's observation in the *Semi-nar* that the experience of the Mother as frustration by the subject, as in Kleinian theory, is an instance of the Thing.

3. "In one of the most important contemporary works on autobiography, Philippe Lejeune (1975) links the form to the linguistic peculiarity of the proper name as such; but the anonymity I mean, the anonymity of that counterauto-biography, which is among other things the testimonial novel, is then in that

sense not the loss of a name, but—quite paradoxically—the multiplication of proper names. 'The Autobiography of Estaban Montejo' [sic], by Miguel Barnet . . . , 'The Life of Rigoberta Menchú [sic], by Elizabeth Burgos-Debray . . .'" (Fredric Jameson, "On Literary and Cultural Import-Substitution in the Third World," in *The Real Thing: Testimonial Discourse and Latin America,* ed. Georg M. Gugelberger [Durham, N.C.: Duke University Press, 1996], 185). "Mastersubject" is from Jameson's interview with Anders Stephanson: "I always insist on a third possibility beyond the old bourgeois ego and the schizophrenic subject of our organization society today: a *collective subject,* decentered but not schizophrenic. It emerges in certain forms of storytelling that can be found in thirdworld literature, in testimonial literature, in gossip and rumors and things of this kind. . . . It is decentered since the stories you tell there as an individual subject don't belong to you; you don't control them in the way the master subject of modernism would. But you don't just suffer them in the schizophrenic isolation of the first-world subject of today" (Anders Stephanson, "Regarding Postmodernism— A Conversation with Fredric Jameson," *Social Text* 17 [1987], 45).

4. Alice Brittin and Kenya Dworkin, "Rigoberta Menchú: 'Los indígenas no nos quedamos como bichos aislados, inmunes, desde hace 500 años. No, nosotros hemos sido protagonistas de la historia,'" *Nuevo Texto Crítico* 6:11 (1993): 214. The issue of authorship in testimonio is often a point of conflict between the parties involved in its production. Thus, for example, in the first, Cuban edition of *Biografía de un cimarrón,* Miguel Barnet appears as the author, even though the text is a first-person narrative, presumably to indicate that he—as a writer— has created a novel-like text (his own formula is *novela-testimonio*) out of the linguistic raw material proffered by his subaltern informant, Esteban Montejo. In the subsequent English translation, now out of print, the work was retitled, more accurately in my opinion, *Autobiography of a Runaway Slave,* the author was designated as Esteban Montejo, and Barnet appeared as the editor. In a new English translation published by Curbstone Press (1995), prepared with Barnet's approval, the book is again titled *Biography of a Runaway Slave* and Barnet again appears as the author.

5. "Figures like the goddess Athena—'father's daughters self-professedly uncontaminated by the womb'—are useful for establishing women's ideological self-debasement, which is to be distinguished from a deconstructive attitude toward the essentialist subject" (Gayatri Chakravorty Spivak, "Can the Subaltern Speak?" in *Marxism and the Interpretation of Culture,* ed. Cary Nelson and Lawrence Grossberg [New York: Routledge, 1988], 308).

6. See in this regard Walter Mignolo's observation (also quoted in chapter 2) about the Spanish practice of segregating the children of the Indian aristocracy from their families in order to teach them literacy and Christianity. The violence of such a practice, he writes, "is not located in the fact that the youngsters have been assembled and enclosed day and night. It comes, rather, from the interdiction of having conversations with their parents, particularly with their mothers. In a primary oral society, in which virtually all knowledge is transmitted by

means of conversation, the preservation of oral contact was contradictory with the effort to teach how to read and write. Forbidding conversations with the mother meant, basically, depriving the children of the living culture imbedded in the language and preserved and transmitted in speech" (Walter Mignolo, "Literacy and Colonization: The New World Experience," in *1482–1992. Re/Discovering Colonial Writing* (Minneapolis: Prisma Institute, 1989), ed. René Jara and Nicholas Spadaccini, 67.

7. Alberto Moreiras, "The Aura of Testimonio," in Gugelberger, *The Real Thing*, 210.

8. "No representa una reacción genuina y espontánea del 'sujeto-pueblo multiforme' frente a la condición postcolonial, sino que sigue siendo un discurso de las élites comprometidas a la causa de la democratización" (Elzbieta Sklodowska, "Hacia una tipología del testimonio hispanoamericano," *Siglo XX/Twentieth Century* 8:1–2 [1990–91]: 113; my translation). The concept of "sujeto-pueblo multiforme" Sklodowska alludes to comes from the Chilean critic Jorge Narváez.

9. It is useful to recall in this respect Menchú's own advice in her testimonio that "Cada uno de nosostros tiene que conocer nuestra realidad y optar por los demás," which I translate loosely as "each of us has to know our own reality, and then (be in a position to) express solidarity with others."

10. See Gayatri Chakravorty Spivak, *In Other Worlds: Essays in Cultural Politics* (New York: Methuen, 1988), 95.

11. I refer here to Spivak's own elaboration of the distinction between *vertreten* and *darstellen* in Marx in "Can the Subaltern Speak?"

12. Ángel Rama, *La ciudad letrada* (Hanover, N.H.: Ediciones del Norte, 1984).

13. Dinesh D'Souza, *Illiberal Education* (New York: Free Press, 1991), 87.

14. According to Pratt, a poll of undergraduate students at Stanford revealed that *I, Rigoberta Menchú* was the book they had found most meaningful in their classes. A similar poll at my institution, the University of Pittsburgh, would produce a different result, in part because Pitt students are from lower-middle-class and working-class backgrounds.

15. Brittin and Dworkin "Rigoberta Menchú," 214.

16. Edward Said, *Culture and Imperialism* (New York: Vintage, 1994).

17. "[T]he historical phenomenon of [peasant] insurgency meets the eye for the first time as an image framed in the prose, hence the outlook, of counter-insurgency—an image caught in a distorting mirror. However, the distortion has a logic to it. That is the logic of opposition between the rebels and their enemies not only as parties engaged in active hostility on a particular occasion but as the mutually antagonistic elements of a semi-feudal society under colonial rule. The antagonism is rooted deeply enough in the material and spiritual conditions of their existence to reduce the difference between elite and subaltern perceptions to a difference between the terms of a binary pair. . . . Inscribed in elite discourse, it [the rebellion] had to be read as a writing in reverse. Since our access to rebel consciousness lay, so to say, through enemy country, we had to seize on

the evidence of elite consciousness and force it to show us the way to its Other" (Ranajit Guha, *Elementary Aspects of Peasant Insurgency in Colonial India* [Delhi: Oxford University Press, 1983], 333).

18. "Yo creo que los indígenas debemos aprovechar y captar todos aquellos valores grandes de los descubrimientos de la ciencia y la tecnología. Hay grandes cosas que han alcanzado la ciencia y la tecnología y no podemos decir: 'los indígenas no vamos a ser parte de esto,' pues de hecho somos parte de ello" (I believe that indians should take advantage of and assimilate all these great values offered by the discoveries of science and technology. Science and technology have accomplished great things and we can't say "we indians aren't going to be a part of that," because in fact we are part of it) (Brittin and Dworkin, "Rigoberta Menchú," 212).

19. Jean-Paul Sartre, *Anti-Semite and Jew,* trans. George Becker (New York: Shocken, 1965).

20. Jacques Lacan, "Tuché and Automaton," in *The Four Fundamental Concepts of Psychoanalysis* (New York: Norton, 1978), 53–66. René Jara has noted that "More than a translation of reality, testimonio is a *trace of the Real,* of that history which, as such, is unrepresentable" ("Prólogo," in *Testimonio y literatura,* ed. René Jara and Hernán Vidal [Minneapolis: Institute for the Study of Ideologies and Literature, 1986], 2–3).

21. Rigoberta Menchú, with Elisabeth Burgos-Debray, *I, Rigoberta Menchú: An Indian Woman in Guatemala,* trans. Ann Wright (London: Verso, 1984), 178–79.

22. This was, of course, the strategy of the antislave narrative produced by Latin American liberal elites or would-be elites in the nineteenth century. It is also a problem with *Schindler's List,* as the emerging critical discussion of the film has begun to register. Spielberg's use of the Schindler story personalizes the Holocaust and brings it closer to the viewer: that was undoubtedly a brilliant stroke by Spielberg and it differentiates his film from a "modernist" treatment of the Holocaust such as Alain Resnais's *Night and Fog.* The price, however, is that the Jews (as a group) can be represented in the film only as victims, dependent on Schindler and on the character played by Ben Kingsley, who allegorizes the role of the traditional Jewish leadership in the *Judenrats,* for their salvation. A Zionist or Communist representation would have critiqued the role of the *Judenrats* and stressed the possibility of Jewish self-organization from below and armed struggle against the Nazi system, instead of their reliance on the benevolence of both Jewish and non-Jewish capitalist-humanist elites. Even the representation of the Holocaust, in other words, is taken away in *Schindler's List* from the actual victims or participants; the film as a capitalist enterprise mirrors Schindler's business venture as the *necessary* vehicle for Jewish salvation. It is interesting to contrast Spielberg's strategy with the collective montage of direct testimonios by Holocaust survivors presented in the Holocaust Museum in Washington.

23. I quote from a manuscript copy that Professor Stoll made available to me of his unpublished paper, "*I, Rigoberta Menchú* and Human Rights Reporting

in Guatemala," presented at a conference on the theme "'Political Correctness' and Cultural Studies" at the University of California Berkeley, October 20, 1990. Without noting the incident of the brother in particular, Stoll makes a similar claim about Menchú in "'The Land No Longer Gives': Land Reform in Nebaj, Guatemala," *Cultural Survival Quarterly* 14:4 (1990): 4–9, especially 4–5). Stoll had been studying the process of evangelization of these communities by U.S.-sponsored fundamentalist Protestant sects, which began during the period described in *I, Rigoberta Menchú,* sometimes, particularly during the presidency of Efraín Ríos Montt, in direct connection with the counterinsurgency campaigns being mounted by the Guatemalan army in the highlands. It is not clear whether in questioning the validity of Menchú's testimonio Stoll's own position is that of an impartial observer, concerned with how the communities became trapped between the military and the guerrillas, or of someone who in one way or another identifies with or supports the evangelization process, in which case he would be predisposed to downplay Menchú because of her connection to Catholic base communities and the guerrillas, who were competing with the fundamentalists for support among these communities. In the same way (and, to my way of thinking at least, with similar political consequences), a social scientist involved with Buthelezi and the project of the Inkatha party might have questioned the claim of Nelson Mandela and the African National Congress to adequately represent black South Africans in general, for example.

24. This was written, of course, in 1996. Subsequently, Stoll repeated the charge in his book *Rigoberta Menchú and the Story of All Poor Guatemalans,* and Menchú, in response, admitted that she was in fact not present at the event, that she narrated it through the eyes of her mother, who was. On this point, see the final essay in this volume, "What Happens When the Subaltern Speaks."

25. Shoshana Felman and Dori Laub, *Testimony: Crises of Witnessing in Literature, Psychoanalysis, and History* (New York and London: Routledge, 1992), 59.

26. John Beverley, *Against Literature* (Minneapolis: University of Minnesota Press, 1993), 97.

27. "Any statement of authority has no other guarantee than its very enunciation, and it is pointless for it to seek another signifier, which could not appear outside this locus in any way. Which is what I mean when I say that no metalanguage can be spoken, or, more aphoristically, that there is no Other of the Other. And when the Legislator (he who claims to lay down the Law) presents himself to fill the gap, he does so as an imposter" (Jacques Lacan, *Écrits: A Selection* [New York: W. W. Norton, 1977], 310–11).

28. See, for example, Beth and Steve Cagan's account of one such community in El Salvador, *This Promised Land, El Salvador* (New Brunswick, N.J., and London: Rutgers University Press, 1991).

29. The *Nuevo Texto Crítico* interview confirms what sources close to Menchú have noted previously: that the basic editing of the transcript was done not only by Elisabeth Burgos but also by a team of Menchú's *compañeros* from the

political organization she was associated with in Guatemala, working together with her in Mexico City after the sessions with Burgos in Paris. In a sense, *I, Rigoberta Menchú* is thus a text produced not only by a committee but by a central committee, with specific political goals in mind.

30. Ranajit Guha offers a brilliant description of such modes of oral discursive construction and transmission in peasant cultures in *Elementary Aspects of Peasant Insurgency*. What is relevant to *I, Rigoberta Menchú* is that the mode of transmission is dependent on the highly socialized character of everyday community life, in which women play a key role.

31. Javier Sanjinés, "Beyond Testimonial Discourse: New Popular Trends in Bolivia," in Gugelberger, *The Real Thing*, 254–65.

32. Fredric Jameson, "On 'Cultural Studies,'" *Social Text* 34 (1993): 17.

4. What Happens When the Subaltern Speaks

1. Rigoberta Menchú, with Elisabeth Burgos, *I, Rigoberta Menchú: An Indian Woman in Guatemala*, trans. Ann Wright (London: Verso, 1984), 178–79.

2. David Stoll, *Rigoberta Menchú and the Story of All Poor Guatemalans* (Boulder, Colo.: Westview Press, 1999), viii.

3. John Beverley, *Against Literature* (Minneapolis: University of Minnesota Press, 1993), 70.

4. Rigoberta Menchú, interview by Juan Jesús Arnárez, "Those Who Attack Me Humiliate the Victims," *El País*, January 24, 1999.

5. For example, in the following passage: "At this point, the identity needs of Rigoberta's academic constituency play into the weakness of rules of evidence in postmodern scholarship. Following the thinking of literary theorists such as Edward Said and Gayatri Spivak, anthropologists have become very interested in problems of narrative, voice, and representation, especially the problem of how we misrepresent voices other than our own. In reaction, some anthropologists argue that the resulting fascination with texts threatens the claim of anthropology to be a science, by replacing hypothesis, evidence, and generalization with stylish forms of introspection" (Stoll 247).

6. Moreover, as he makes clear at the end of his book, Stoll intends not only a *retrospective* critique of armed struggle in Guatemala; he also means his book as a caution against enthusiasm for contemporary armed struggle movements such as the Zapatistas in Mexico (see, e.g., 279–80). Indeed, for Stoll rural guerrilla strategies *as such* "are an urban romance, a myth propounded by middle-class radicals who dream of finding true solidarity in the countryside"; such strategies have "repeatedly been fatal for the left itself, by dismaying lower-class constituents and guaranteeing a crushing response from the state" (282). The "mythic inflation" or simplification of indigenous life and rural realities that *I, Rigoberta Menchú* supposedly performs colludes with this urban romance.

7. My own view is that under conditions of military and paramilitary rule in which even the most cautious ladino trade unionists and social-democratic or Christian Democratic elected officials were likely to be "disappeared," and in

the context of the Sandinista victory in 1979, it is not surprising that armed resistance came to seem to many people in Guatemala as a desperate but plausible strategy.

8. See Carol A. Smith, "Why Write an Exposé of Rigoberta Menchú?" in *The Rigoberta Menchú Controversy*, ed. Arturo Arias (Minneapolis: University of Minnesota Press, 2001), 141–55.

9. To give credit where credit is due, the point about "other" narratives of Guatemalan indigenous life that contradict or relativize aspects of Menchú's *testimonio* was first made by Marc Zimmerman, in his essay "El otro de Rigoberta," in *La voz del otro: Testimonio, subalternidad y verdad narrativa*, ed. John Beverley and Hugo Achugar (Pittsburgh and Lima: Latinoamerica Editores, 1992), 229–43.

10. Charles Taylor, "The Politics of Recognition," in *Multiculturalism: Examining the Politics of Recognition*, ed. Amy Gutman (Princeton, N.J.: Princeton University Press, 1994).

11. Homi Bhabha, "Editor's Introduction," *Front Lines/Border Posts*, a special issue of *Critical Inquiry* 23:3 (1997): 458–60.

12. Mario Roberto Morales, *La articulación de las diferencias: El debate inter étnico en Guatemala* (Guatemala City: FLACSO, 1999). See also his essay "Menchú after Stoll and the Truth Commission," in Arias, *The Rigoberta Menchú Controversy*, 351–71.

13. Like many Central American intellectuals of his generation, Morales condenses in his own person and career the intersection of these two forms of practice. In the 1970s and 1980s, he was a cadre in one of the organizations that protagonized the armed struggle in Guatemala, an experience he describes in his tragicomic memoir *Los que se fueron por la libre* (1998). At the same time, he was becoming known as an emerging voice in Guatemalan literature in a series of novels that touched on the political crisis his generation of middle-class youth experienced: *Los demonios salvajes* (1977), *El esplendor de la pirámide* (1986), *Señores baja los árboles* (1994), and *El ángel de la retaguardia* (1997). His first book of literary criticism, *La ideología y la lírica de la lucha armada* (1992), along with the book Marc Zimmerman and I coauthored, *Literature and Politics in the Central American Revolutions* (1990), was one of the most rigorous efforts to theorize the relationship between revolutionary militancy and the new forms of Latin American literature coming out of vanguardism and the Boom.

14. Ángel Rama, *Transculturación narrativa en América Latina* (Mexico City: Siglo XXI, 1982).

15. Wendy Brown has analyzed acutely the political impasse that identity politics may lead to (I am indebted to Gareth Williams for bringing this passage to my attention): "In its emergence as a protest against marginalization or subordination, politicized identity . . . becomes attached to its own exclusion both because it is premised on this exclusion for its existence as identity and because the identity as the site of exclusion, as exclusion, augments or 'alters the direction

of the suffering' entailed in subordination or marginalization by finding a site of blame for it. But in so doing, it installs pain over its unredeemed history in the very foundation of its political claim, in its demand for recognition as identity. In locating a site of blame for its powerlessness over its past—a past of injury, a past as a hurt will—and locating a 'reason' for the 'unendurable pain' of social power-lessness in the present, it converts this reasoning into an ethnicizing politics, a politics of recrimination that seeks to avenge the hurt even while it reaffirms it, discursively codifies it. Politicized identity thus enunciates itself, makes claims for itself, only by entrenching, restating, dramatizing, and inscribing its pain in politics; it can hold out no future—for itself or others—that triumphs over this pain. The loss of historical direction, and with it the loss of futurity character-istic of the late modern age, is thus homologically refigured in the structure of desire of the dominant political expression of the age: identity politics" (Wendy Brown, *State of Injury: Power and Freedom in Late Modernity* [Princeton, N.J.: Princeton University Press, 1995], 73–74). The point is well taken, and coincides with Morales's skepticism about Mayan identity politics in Guatemala. But, like Morales, Brown presupposes that identity politics cannot aspire to become hege-monic without losing its raison d'être, that subaltern negativity can only affirm impotence, resentment, and suffering. One thing is identity politics without the transformative possibility of hegemony—that is, within the "rules of the game" of the dominant class and political-legal institutions (Brown notes in this respect that identity politics paradoxically runs the risk of becoming "a protest that . . . reinstalls the humanist ideal [of the inclusive/universal community] so far as it premises itself on an exclusion from it" [65]); another—what Ernesto Laclau and Chantal Mouffe are trying to point to in their notion of the "egalitarian imagi-nary" as the articulating principle of a new kind of popular-democratic alliance politics—is identity politics with that possibility, since, by definition, even the prospect of attaining hegemony would necessarily transform the identities that enter into play in a process of hegemonic articulation to start with. But if the subaltern has to become like *that which is already hegemonic* in order to become itself hegemonic, then what will have been gained? Obviously, *something* of its initial "identity" as subaltern, marginal, excluded would have to be present in any new discursive structure or *combinatoire* of hegemony. It cannot enter into politics simply by renouncing or "deconstructing" its identity claims without also affirming a fictive universalism or "humanism." Laclau and Mouffe note that "[t]he original forms of democratic thought were linked to a positive and unified conception of human nature," whereas identity politics confronts us with "the emergence of a *plurality of subjects,* whose form of constitution and diver-sity it is only possible to think if we relinquish the category of the 'subject' as a unified and unifying essence" (Ernesto Laclau and Chantal Mouffe, *Hegemony and Socialist Strategy* [London: Verso, 1995], 180–81). But is not "democratic thought" itself a class- and ethnically specific form of thought (the thought of the European bourgeoisie in its struggle against feudal power), and is not *all* politics in this sense identity politics?

16. As a graduate student in my department noted apropos the Stoll–Menchú debate, the question is not Can the subaltern speak? but Can the subaltern speak in a way that manipulates or dupes us to serve her interests?

17. Ranajit Guha, "The Prose of Counter-Insurgency," in *Selected Subaltern Studies,* ed. Ranajit Guha and Gayatri Spivak (New York: Oxford University Press, 1988). I am indebted to José Rabasa for this observation.

Index

John Beverley is professor and chair of the Department of Hispanic Languages and Literatures at the University of Pittsburgh. His books include *Against Literature* (Minnesota, 1993) and *Subalternity and Representation.*